THE MIZZOU FAN'S
SURVIVAL GUIDE TO THE SEC

Ron Higgins   Steve Richardson   Dave Matter

REEDY PRESS
St. Louis, Missouri

Reedy Press
PO Box 5131
St. Louis, MO 63139, USA

Library of Congress Control Number: 2012938349

ISBN: 978-1-935806-28-8

Please visit our website at www.reedypress.com.

Cover design by Rob Staggenborg
Interior design by Jill Halpin
Top cover photo courtesy Mizzou Athletics Media Relations

Printed in the United States of America
12 13 14 15 16   5 4 3 2 1

CONTENTS

PREFACE

The move to the Southeastern Conference is on!

With the University of Missouri's athletic programs jumping into the SEC in the fall of 2012, Tiger fans will encounter a "new frontier" of competition after 105 years of facing schools in the Missouri Valley, Big Six, Big Seven, Big Eight, and finally Big 12 conferences.

The familiar trips to Lawrence, Manhattan, Ames, Norman, Stillwater, etc., give way to new destinations such as Gainesville, Knoxville, and Columbia, S.C., in the inaugural year in football and several other locales in other sports. Eventually, over a period of years, Mizzou will play a football game on every SEC campus.

Thus, there is a need for an information source for Tiger fans who follow their team to the new towns and cities: *The Mizzou Fan's Survival Guide to the SEC.* While this book focuses mostly on what to do on college football weekends, it can be applied to any of the cities where the Tigers compete in SEC play in other sports.

There may not be a more diverse state in this country than Missouri, which was a border state during the Civil War. Tiger fans must realize that culturally in some parts of the state they never have been really that far from the SEC. Three states with SEC schools (Arkansas, Kentucky, and Tennessee) are contiguous with the state of Missouri. Columbia has often been referred to as "Little Dixie" because of its historical leanings to the Confederacy and the tobacco and hemp plantations in the region.

That being said, rivalries with SEC schools have been spotty over the years, even with the schools located in the border states. Arkansas and Missouri, for instance, have not played a regular-season game since 1963, although they have met in two bowls (Independence and Cotton) during the last decade. Tennessee and Missouri have never faced each other on the football field. The Tigers haven't played Vanderbilt since 1958. And Kentucky and Missouri last met each other in football in 1968. Missouri has played each of the other nine schools in football sometime in its history, but the Tigers have played only Mississippi and, of course, Texas A&M during the regular season since the beginning of the new millennium.

Tips to finding a place to stay, grabbing a snack, sitting down for a meal, shopping, or sightseeing are included in this book, as well as tailgating procedures, important phone numbers and addresses, and how to get to the new locales from the state of Missouri. There are tidbits about each school's football history, other notable sports, and famous alumni, along with various other items on the school's culture and traditions. Each school also has connections to the University of Missouri over the years that are mentioned in each school's section.

Missouri and Texas A&M also will be hosting SEC fans for the first time on a regular basis in 2012 in several sports. So the sections on the Tigers and Aggies should be of interest to the general SEC fans from the other twelve league schools.

The 2012 football season—starting with the SEC league games of September 8—should be a unique and memorable experience for Mizzou fans everywhere. On that day, Missouri opens SEC play with a home game against defending SEC East Division champion Georgia. Missouri fans can chant "M-I-Z S-E-C" with pride and distinction. And, as they prepare for the rest of this inaugural season, this handy resource guide can make their journey to the Land of Dixie easier.

—Ron Higgins, Dave Matter, Steve Richardson
March 2012

ABOUT THE SEC

It must have been some meeting.

When the twenty-three-member Southern Conference held its annual business meeting in Knoxville on December 9, 1932, everybody wasn't exactly holding hands. In fact, thirteen members had decided they'd had enough of being in a league that stretched from Louisiana to Maryland.

The geographical distance was too hard on travel budgets, not to mention travel time for athletes. There was also a big gap in athletic commitment from large and small schools in the league. Scheduling was a nightmare, since teams in such a huge conference had no chance of playing each other, even over a period of several years.

That December night in Knoxville, then-Florida president John J. Tigert announced that his institution and twelve other schools in the Southern Conference located west and south of the Appalachian Mountains were jumping ship to form a new league—the Southeastern Conference.

When the SEC opened for business in 1933, its members included Alabama, Auburn, Florida, Georgia, Georgia Tech, Kentucky, LSU, Ole Miss, Mississippi State, Sewanee, Tennessee, Tulane, and Vanderbilt.

The league went without organized leadership until 1940 when former Mississippi governor Martin S. Conner became commissioner. He established the league office in Jackson, Mississippi, but the conference headquarters moved to Birmingham in 1948, where it has stayed since.

Over the years, the SEC has subtracted three members and added four. Sewanee left in 1940, because its religious administration decided to deemphasize athletics. Georgia Tech withdrew in 1940, because football coach

Bobby Dodd thought the league let football recruiting get out of control. Tulane, the only other private school in the conference besides Vanderbilt, left in 1966, because it simply wasn't competitive.

The SEC stayed a ten-team league all the way until 1992, when Arkansas of the Southwest Conference and independent South Carolina joined. And that's when the SEC, with twelve teams in two six-team divisions playing a league championship football game for the first time, began its ascent as a predominant athletic monster.

Adding Arkansas and South Carolina made the SEC a more desirable TV property. So when CBS signed its first contract with the SEC in 1994, league revenue sharing jumped from $16.3 million in 1990 to $40.3 million in 1995.

More revenue from each school meant more money being poured back into programs for better facilities and coaches. The more a school wins, the more money an athletic program can raise to feed the flame of excellence. The more schools win national championships and compete on a national level, the more it can demand from TV networks an increase in revenue and number of exposures, the latter of which accelerates recruiting to keep the product at a high level.

In August 2008, most of the other BCS conferences gulped when the SEC signed fifteen-year agreements with CBS and ESPN starting in 2009-10— contracts worth a combined $3 billion for more than 5,500 events on all the ESPN platforms.

Since the 1992 expansion, the league has won:

- Ten national championships in football, including a current string of six straight, by five different schools. This past season, the SEC had three teams finish in the top three of the Associated Press poll (No. 1 Alabama, No. 2 LSU, No. 5 Arkansas) for the second time in history.

- Five men's NCAA basketball titles by three schools, in addition to thirteen teams in the Final Four, including two in the same year three times (1994, 1996, 2006).
- Seven College World Series (including the last two, both by South Carolina), with ten of twelve SEC schools playing in at least one CWS, and five CWS that had three or more SEC schools in the field.
- Five women's NCAA basketball championships (all by Tennessee) with twenty-two Final Four appearances by six different schools.

Since 1992, the SEC has won fifty-nine national women's team titles in eleven different sports and seventy-two NCAA men's team championships in nine sports. The league's exceedingly hot run in the major sports (football, men's and women's basketball, and baseball)—a combined fifteen national titles since 2000—upped the TV ante even more.

In June 2011, the SEC broke its revenue-sharing record for the twenty-first consecutive year, distributing a record $220 million among its twelve schools, an average of $18.3 million per school.

Now that the SEC is expanding again, adding Missouri and Texas A&M, expect the TV money to rise. Former Arkansas football coach and athletic director Frank Broyles says both new SEC schools will realize switching leagues is the best decision they ever made. "I hate to even think where we'd be had we not joined the SEC," says Broyles, who retired in December 2007 after sixteen years as head football coach, three as head coach and athletic director, and thirty-one as athletic director. "There's not a selfish program in the conference. We're what you call 'team players.' We recognize when you're team players, everybody prospers."

Broyles says the fervor for SEC sports is unrivaled, a combination of the South's love for college sports and simple geography. For instance, Arkansas touches the borders of Louisiana, Texas, Missouri, Mississippi, and Tennessee. Such location, location, location amps up the SEC, says Broyles. All of the states with SEC schools are connected to each other. "When you're neighbors with each other, competition is natural," Broyles says. "You don't have to build competition interest, because there's built-in arguing already. The people next door don't like you. The SEC has border rivalries, and border rivalries are bitter. They argue and compete year-round."

Considering that Missouri and Texas A&M are coming from a league (the Big 12) with six of ten members having home football stadiums with 62,000 seats or fewer, to a conference with eight schools playing on home fields with 80,000 seats or more, there might be an adjustment period for the newbies.

"Adding Missouri and Texas A&M will make the conference more competitive," says retired SEC commissioner Roy Kramer, who was the father of the 1992 expansion and who helped create the BCS. "It will create new rivalries and fans, and gives the league's TV partners more exposure. But there will be some instant cultural growing up for Missouri and A&M, because there's a passion in this part of the country I'm not sure they've seen."

That's true. The SEC, which turns eighty this year, is a bit different, because in this crazy league:

- Roll Tide, War Eagle, Hunker Down Hairy Dawgs, and Geaux Tigers are acceptable substitutes for hello.

- Five-star dining can be on a grill under a tent in the Grove at Ole Miss, a spread of hors d'oeuvres on a white tablecloth on a boat on Lake Loudon outside of Tennessee's Neyland Stadium, or next to a crawfish boiler in a Tiger Stadium parking lot at LSU.

- There aren't many statues of war heroes or college founders on campuses. But there are statues of Heisman Trophy winners or football coaches who have won national championships.

· A cowbell is a fashion accessory, like at Mississippi State, where an SEC rule allows Bulldogs' fans to clank them between plays.

· Sunday is a day of worship and reflection for SEC fans, meaning you pray your head coach gets fired because you've been obsessing about why he never changes his predictable offense.

· Season football tickets are often a major point of contention dividing property in divorce proceedings.

· January means bowls, February is signing day, March and April are spring practice, May means preseason magazines hit the stands, June is hoping your star player doesn't get arrested, July is for buying a new cap for the season, August is preseason practice, September through November is bowl bliss or bust, and December is firing and hiring of new coaches.

· SEC fans can't tell you the exact date that man first walked on the moon, but they can tell you that former Alabama quarterback Joe Namath's middle name is Willie, that Steve Spurrier is the only person ever to win the Heisman Trophy as a player and later guide a team to a national championship as a coach, and that LSU's Billy Cannon's famous eighty-nine-yard TD punt return on Halloween night 1959 against Ole Miss is arguably the greatest play in league history.

· The father, the sons, and the Holy Ghost are former Ole Miss quarterback Archie Manning, Super Bowl championship quarterback sons Peyton (who played for Tennessee) and Eli (who played for Ole Miss), and the late Ole Miss coach Johnny Vaught, who coached Archie.

· Fans of some rival schools might not ever totally like each other (Alabama–Auburn, Ole Miss–Mississippi State), but when SEC teams play in bowls or in the NCAA basketball tournament, the College World Series—anything involving the SEC vs. the rest of the nation—fans at each institution have fierce league pride.

True story: The night before the 2011 Sugar Bowl in New Orleans between Arkansas of the SEC and Ohio State of the Big Ten, a couple of inebriated fans from each team began fighting each other on Bourbon Street. Before the police broke it up, the Arkansas fan began winning the fight. As he gained the upper hand, the crowd that gathered to witness the brawl began chanting "S-E-C, S-E-C, S-E-C!"

That might be extreme to the rest of the country, but it's how the SEC rolls.

Welcome to the family, Mizzou. Get out your boxing gloves and start swinging.

ALABAMA

If the Confederate Army could have defended the University of Alabama campus from Union forces on April 4, 1865, half as well as the Crimson Tide defense stopped LSU in 2012's BCS championship game, then the UA would not have had to re-build most of its buildings after the Union Army torched them in the Civil War.

The Union Army's visit happened thirty-four years after the university opened its doors for operation on April 18, 1831, just twelve years after Alabama was granted statehood. Once the university re-opened in 1871 and added a law school a year later, it got back on track. It made the bold step of admitting women students in 1893, but enrollment didn't skyrocket until Dr. George Denny became the UA's president in 1912. UA went through some well-documented racial strife when, in 1956, the school admitted Autherine J. Lucy, its first African-American student. Fearing for her safety, school officials expelled her after three days. Lucy eventually received a degree from Alabama in 1992. The first sustained enrollment of African-American students at the UA—Vivian J. Malone and James A. Hood—was achieved in 1961.

UNIVERSITY OF ALABAMA

Students: 31,747

Tuscaloosa: pop. 90,468

Bryant-Denny Stadium: seats 101,821

Colors: Crimson and White

Nickname: Crimson Tide

Mascot: Big Al

Campus Attractions: Denny Chimes, President's Mansion

Phone: 205-348-6010 (general information)
205-348-5454 (campus police)
205-348-3600 (athletic department)

Tickets: 205-348-2262 or ticketoffice@ia.ua.edu

In 1969, Alabama signed its first African-American athlete—basketball player Wendell Hudson—who today is the Crimson Tide's women's head basketball coach. Shortly thereafter in 1971, legendary Tide football coach Bear Bryant signed his first African-American player, John Mitchell of Mobile, who later became the first African-American football assistant at Alabama under Bryant.

Adding black athletes made a good football program great. Even before the SEC officially became a conference, Alabama, which began playing football in 1892, was steps ahead of the rest of Southern football. UA was the first SEC team to play in the Rose Bowl, edging unbeaten Washington, 20-19, in 1926.

When Bryant returned to Alabama from Texas A&M in 1958—"Mama called," he always said of why he left A&M for Tuscaloosa—it took him just four seasons to win the first of his six national championships. One of Bryant's secrets was never being afraid to re-invent himself, such as ditching the Tide's pro-style offense after a disappointing 1970 season and installing the wishbone offense invented by Emory Bellard (who later coached at Mississippi State) and made popular by the University of Texas. Because of the wishbone, Bryant was able to win the final three national championships of his career in 1973, 1978, and 1979. Twenty-eight days after Bryant retired from coaching, winning his final game in the Liberty Bowl, he died at sixty-nine on January 26, 1983.

Since then, Alabama has gone through eight coaches (one was fired before even coaching a game). Gene Stallings, who played for Bryant at Texas A&M in the 1950s and whose deep Southern drawl was reminiscent of his mentor, guided the Tide to a 13-0 record and a 1992 national championship.

After the 2006 season when Alabama athletic director Mal Moore was shopping for a new coach, he boarded a private university plane bound for Miami, with the thought he wasn't returning to Tuscaloosa until he had persuaded Miami Dolphins head coach Nick Saban to guide the Tide.

PROGRAM HIGHLIGHTS

NATIONAL CHAMPIONSHIPS (14): 1925, 1926, 1930, 1934, 1941, 1961, 1964, 1965, 1973, 1978, 1979, 1992, 2009, 2011

SEC CHAMPIONSHIPS (23): 1933, 1934, 1937, 1945, 1953, 1961, 1964, 1965, 1966, 1971, 1972, 1973, 1974, 1975, 1977, 1978, 1979, 1982, 1989, 1992, 1999, 2009, 2011

BOWL RECORD: 33-22-3 (.595). Last bowl—21-0 over LSU in 2012 BCS national championship game

LONGEST WINNING STREAK: 28 games (twice), 1991-93, 1978-80

WINNINGEST COACH: Paul "Bear" Bryant (1958-82), 232-46-9, 82.4 percent

HEISMAN TROPHY WINNERS OR HIGHEST HEISMAN FINISH: Running back Mark Ingram, 2009 winner

Saban, who won the 2003 BCS title coaching LSU, agreed to return to the college ranks, much to the chagrin of LSU fans. In two of the last three years, Saban and Alabama have won the national championship, making him the only coach in college football history to win national championships at different schools. All of Alabama's coaches recognized for winning a national championship—Wallace Wade, Frank Thomas, Bryant, Stallings, and Saban— have been honored with statues outside of Bryant-Denny Stadium.

LEGENDS

Paul "Bear" Bryant

Regarded as the greatest Southern college coach, if not the best college coach, in history, Bear Bryant helmed six national championship teams at Alabama. His fourteen SEC championships as a head coach (thirteen for Alabama and one for Kentucky in 1950) is an untouchable SEC record.

Lee Roy Jordan

One of the best linebackers in SEC history who had thirty-one tackles against Oklahoma in the 1963 Orange Bowl, Jordan went on to play fourteen seasons for the Dallas Cowboys, where he played in three Super Bowls.

Harry Gilmer

Probably the best all-around player in Tide history, Gilmer finished fifth in Heisman Trophy voting twice in 1945 and 1947.

Joe Namath

Namath wasn't Alabama's best quarterback, but he had a quick-release throwing motion that gave him confidence and panache. He threw for just more than 2,700 career yards and 25 TDs from 1962 to 1964 for Alabama, but "Broadway Joe" attained legend status by guaranteeing the New York Jets' win over the Colts in the third Super Bowl.

STADIUM

Bryant-Denny: The stadium opened in 1929 and was originally named Denny Stadium in honor of former Alabama president George Denny. The stadium's name was amended to Bryant-Denny Stadium in 1975 after the Alabama Legislature chose to honor famed Tide coach Paul "Bear" Bryant, who, by the way, had a record of 72-2 in Bryant-Denny.

NOTABLE ALUMS

Sela Ward—TV and movie actress

Winston Groom—Novelist, wrote *Forrest Gump*

Mel Allen—Late radio play-by-play announcer of the New York Yankees

Jimmy Wales—Co-founder of Wikipedia

FIGHT SONG

"YEA ALABAMA"

Yea Alabama! Drown 'em Tide, Every 'Bama man's behind you, Hit your stride . . .

Go teach the Bulldogs to behave, Send the Yellow Jackets to a watery grave,

And if a man starts to weaken, That's a shame,

Cause 'Bama's pluck and grit have, Writ her name in Crimson Flame,

Fight on, Fight on, Fight on, men! Remember the Rose Bowl we'll win then.

Go, roll to victory, Hit your stride! You're Dixie's football pride, Crimson Tide!

MASCOT

"Big Al," a name chosen by a vote of the Alabama student body, is Alabama's costumed elephant mascot that made his sideline debut at the 1979 Sugar Bowl when 'Bama beat Penn State for the national championship. But the origin of Alabama being known as the "Red Elephants" dates back to October 8, 1930, when *Atlanta Journal* sportswriter Everett Strupper wrote a story on a 64-0 Alabama blowout of Ole Miss that he watched four days earlier. Strupper wrote of Alabama's physical team, "At the end of the (first) quarter, the earth started to tremble, there was a distant rumble that continued to grow. Some excited fan in the stands bellowed, 'Hold your horses, the elephants are coming.'"

MIZZOU CONNECTION

All-time football record vs. Missouri: 1-2

1968: Missouri 35, Alabama 10 (Gator Bowl, Jacksonville, Fla.)

1975: Missouri 20, Alabama 10 (Birmingham)

1978: Alabama 38, Missouri 20 (Columbia)

In the 1968 Gator Bowl, Dan Devine defeated fellow future College Football Hall of Famer Bear Bryant as his Tigers outgained Bryant's Tide 402-32 without attempting a single pass. "They ran up and down the field just as though they were playing a barber's college," Bryant said, as quoted in Bob Broeg's *Ol Mizzou: A Century of Tiger Football*. In 1975, Alabama was ranked No. 2 when Missouri came to Birmingham for a Monday night season opener. Again, it was no contest. "All in all, it was a good ol' sound country beating," Bryant was quoted in the *Columbia Daily Tribune*. Bryant exacted revenge in 1978, killing the buzz of Missouri's upset of Notre Dame the week before.

Teammates reunited: Kent State was the site of tragedy in 1970 with the fatal shooting of four student protestors. Two years later, the football team delivered some much-needed joy with the school's first Mid-American Conference championship. On the roster were two future coaches who will square off in the SEC: Missouri's Gary Pinkel and Alabama's Nick Saban. Saban was a senior safety, while Pinkel was a sophomore tight end. Their lives would intersect again almost twenty years later. Saban spent the 1990 season as Toledo's head coach before leaving for the NFL. On the way out, he recommended an old college teammate for the top Toledo post: Pinkel, the offensive coordinator at Washington. Pinkel got the job, spent a decade at Toledo, then took over at Missouri in 2001. "Gary's a great friend," Saban said after Missouri announced plans to join the SEC in November 2011. "And he was a hell of a lot better player than I was."

Tiger-Tide links: Long before Bryant led the Tide, Thomas Kelly was 'Bama's head coach, going 17-7 from 1915 to 1917. He would resurface five years later—as Missouri's head coach in 1922, coaching the Tigers to a 5-3 record. . . . Derrick Thomas won the Butkus Award at Alabama in 1988 and became an NFL Hall of Famer. His son Derrion Thomas, a prep swimming star in Kansas City, joined the Missouri roster as a walk-on defensive end in 2011. . . . When the voters for the Pro Football Hall of Fame selected the NFL's 1980s All-Decade Team, they went with Kellen Winslow (Missouri) as the No. 1 tight end and Ozzie Newsome (Alabama) as the No. 2 choice.

GAME DAY

MEDIA

Broadcasting the Game: WJOX-FM 94.5 and WJOX-AM 690 in Birmingham, along with WFFN-FM 95.3 and WTSK-AM 790 in Tuscaloosa

Covering the Tide: www.al.com/alabamafootball/ (*Birmingham News, Mobile Register*), www.tidesports.com (*Tuscaloosa News*)

TAILGATING

The best spot on campus to tailgate is the Quad in the heart of campus, but there are rules to be followed. Any group that wants to have a planned tailgating or a game-day event that requires a tent larger than 10′ x 10′ or a secured space must fill out a UA Grounds Use Permit *www.uafacilities.ua.edu/ grounds/pages/grounds-use-permit.htm*. No tents larger than 20′ x 30′ will be allowed on the Quad. No corporate signage may be displayed outside tents. Since classes run until 6 p.m. on Fridays, refrain from taping off or setting up tailgate sites in areas off the Quad until Friday.

SHUTTLE

There's a free-of-charge parking deck with more than four hundred spaces located on 23rd Avenue between 6th and 7th streets, just behind City Hall, between University Boulevard and Bryant Drive. Tuscaloosa Transit runs sixteen buses from this location to Bryant-Denny Stadium, starting three hours prior to game time. The cost to ride the bus (per trip) is $1 for adults, free for children three years and under and 50 cents for senior citizens age sixty or over and people with disabilities.

Other free off-campus parking with shuttles:
University Mall located on McFarland Boulevard and 15th Street for $10 roundtrip per person; the downtown lot at the corner of Greensboro Avenue and Jack Warner Parkway; Central High School, located on 15th Street; DCH Hospital, located at the corner of Bryant Drive and 5th Avenue; Tuscaloosa Magnet School located off McFarland Boulevard and Campus Drive East.

TRADITIONS

The Million Dollar Band: Alabama boasts a 330-member-plus marching band, which was founded in 1913 with fourteen members under the direction of Dr. Gustav Wittig. In 2003, the Million Dollar Band became the twenty-second band to be honored with the Sudle Trophy, an award given by the Sousa Foundation that recognizes "collegiate marching bands of particular excellence that have made outstanding contributions to the American way of life."

Rammer Jammer Cheer: This traditional cheer is now played at the end of games when Alabama has victory in hand. The lyrics originate from *The Rammer-Jammer*, a student newspaper in the 1920s, and the yellowhammer, Alabama's state bird. The cheer goes like this (subbing in Alabama's opponent of the week): *Hey Missouri! Hey Missouri! Hey Missouri! We just beat the hell out of you! Rammer Jammer, Yellowhammer, gave 'em hell, Alabama!*

B-BALL, ETC.

Alabama's men's basketball team has never made it to the Final Four. This fact is amazing considering how many great NBA players Alabama has produced. Robert Horry is the most notable. He won seven NBA championship rings with three teams (two with the Houston Rockets, three with the Los Angeles Lakers, two with the San Antonio Spurs). The big sport in Tuscaloosa besides football, and this may shock you, is women's gymnastics, which has won five national championships (the last one in 2011), all under Coach Sarah Patterson, one of the best SEC coaches in history in any sport.

ABOUT TOWN

Tuscaloosa was the state capital of Alabama from 1826 to 1846, until the capital moved to Montgomery. The population and economy of Tuscaloosa declined until the establishment of the Bryce State Hospital for the Insane helped restore the city's fortunes in the 1850s. The city got another economic boost when Mercedes-Benz opened a plant in 1997 twenty miles east of downtown Tuscaloosa in Vance. Located on the Black Warrior River, Tuscaloosa is the fifth-largest city in Alabama, with a population of 90,468 (according to the 2010 census).

LODGING

The Yellowhammer Inn and Conference Center: This hotel has just fifty-seven rooms in a serene setting between Lake Tuscaloosa and North River Yacht Club. Whether you tour the inn's six-acre garden or visit the spa, this is a hotel that seems like anything but a hotel. *2700 Yacht Club Way NE, Tuscaloosa, AL 35406, 205-343-4215, www.yellowhammerinn.com*

Hotel Capstone: Located on the University of Alabama's campus, next to the Bear Bryant Museum and across from Coleman Coliseum, it has top-of-the-line accommodations featuring the best beds and large flat-screen TVs. *320 Paul Bryant Dr., Tuscaloosa, AL 35401, 205-752-3200, www.hotelcapstone.com*

The city of Tuscaloosa has limited hotel space. The best bet is to stay in Birmingham or one of its suburbs, such as Hoover, where the Galleria, the largest shopping mall in the state, has one hotel attached to it—**The Wynfrey** (*www.wynfrey.com, 800-996-3739*), which is the annual home of the SEC football preseason media days in July—and plenty of other hotels surrounding it. One warning though—game-day traffic from the Birmingham area to Tuscaloosa (fifty-eight miles) just crawls.

EATING

Dreamland: This barbeque joint opened in 1958 when Bear Bryant rolled into Tuscaloosa. It has the basics people love—ribs, sauce, white bread, slaw, beans, and banana pudding. That's it, but that's all you'll need. *5535 15th Ave., East Tuscaloosa, AL 35405, 205-758-8135, www.dreamlandbbq.com*

Nick's in the Sticks: Way off the beaten-path—it could be the official restaurant of anyone in witness protection—this tiny, unpretentious steakhouse packs a big punch without taking a huge bite out of your wallet. *4018 Culver Rd., Tuscaloosa, AL 35401, 205-758-9316*

Bob Baumhower's Wings Sports Grille: Who knew that a former Alabama football star and six-time All-Pro with the Dolphins would be the King of Chicken Wings when he started in the restaurant biz in 1981? Baumhower's is a classic sports bar yet has an extensive affordable menu. *500 Harper Lee Dr., Tuscaloosa, AL 35404, 205-556-5658, www.baumhowers.com*

SIGHTSEEING

Paul W. Bryant Museum: Everything you ever wanted to know and see about the legendary Alabama coach is right here. There's even a Waterford Crystal houndstooth hat that commemorates the Bear's favorite choice of headwear. Open daily from 9 a.m. to 4 p.m., closes on major holidays. Admission is $2 for adults and $1 for senior citizens and children ages six to seventeen. All children under six, alumni association members, UA faculty, and UA students are granted free admission. *300 Paul W. Bryant Dr., Tuscaloosa, AL 35487, 205-348-4668, www.bryantmuseum.com*

***Bama Belle* Riverboat:** A modern-day replica of a paddlewheel riverboat, the *Bama Belle* cruises the Black Warrior River in the heart of Tuscaloosa. There are often dinner cruises on Saturdays, depending on the time of year. *1 Greensboro Ave., Tuscaloosa, AL 35480, 205-339-1108, www.bamabelle.com*

SHOPPING

Prose and Palaver: If you love women's vintage clothing, stop in at Prose and Palaver, a place where you can find the funkiest 1960s clothes and jewelry. *2312-B 6th St., Tuscaloosa, AL 35401, www.proseandpalaver.com*

Bama Fever: You can get every University of Alabama item under the sun at Bama Fever, located in the Midtown Village shopping community. If you can't find your UA item here, then you just can't find it. *1800 McFarland Blvd., Ste. 604, Tuscaloosa, AL 35404, 205-409-2705, www.bamafever.com*

NIGHTLIFE

Houndstooth Sports Bar: This watering hole was once named the nation's No. 1 college sports bar by *Sports Illustrated*. Maybe it's because of the forty flatscreen TVs (even in the bathroom while you're doing your business). *1300 University Blvd., Tuscaloosa, AL 35401, 205-752-8444, www.houndstoothsportsbar.com*

Harry's Bar: Established in 1972 by former Alabama football player Harry Hammond, this is a loveable dive where you write your name on the wall to let all future generations know that you once passed out at Harry's. *1330 Hargrove Rd., Tuscaloosa, AL 35401, 205-758-9332*

Jupiter Bar and Grill: Jupiter has a better-than-average menu, plus a wide selection of live musical acts. Better yet, a new Waffle House opened next door about a month after Alabama beat LSU in the BCS national championship game. *1307 University Blvd., Tuscaloosa, AL 35401, 205-248-6611*

TRAVELING TO TUSCALOOSA?

It's a quick hour's drive from Birmingham-Shuttlesworth International to Alabama's campus in Tuscaloosa. Columbia Regional Airport offers regular service through Memphis International, where you can pick up a connection to Birmingham. Alabama is about a ten-hour drive from Columbia, eight from St. Louis, and twelve from Kansas City. The Mizzou Alumni Association hosts a Tiger Tailgate. Visit MizzouSportsTravel.com for more information on tickets and pricing.

ARKANSAS

Washington County, where Fayetteville is located, produced the best bid in the state in 1871 to locate Arkansas Industrial University within its boundaries. The first classes were held in 1872. Old Main was built in 1875 and is one of eleven buildings on campus named to the National Register of Historic Places. In 1899, the University of Arkansas name was adopted.

The "great building program of 1905" spurred expansion of the campus, and by 1928 there were twenty-five buildings. By 2005, 130 buildings dotted the 345-acre university. Arkansas was the first major public university in the South to admit an African-American student without litigation. Silas Hunt was admitted to the University of Arkansas law school in 1948, but he died a year later of tuberculosis before he could obtain a degree.

UNIVERSITY OF ARKANSAS

Students: 21,406

Fayetteville: pop. 73,580

Donald W. Reynolds Stadium: seats 72,000

Colors: Cardinal and White

Nickname: Razorbacks

Mascot: Tusk I, Big Red, Sue E, Pork Chop, Boss Hog

Campus Attractions: Old Main, the first building on campus was completed in 1875; Chi Omega Greek Theater, an amphitheater dating to 1930.

Phone: 479-575-5346 (general information)
479-575-2222 (campus police)
479-575-2751 (athletic department)

Tickets: 479-575-5151 or toll-free: 800-982-4647
raztk@uark.edu

Athletically, Arkansas was a longtime member of the Southwest Conference starting in 1915 under Coach T. T. McConnell. But the Razorbacks didn't win their first outright SWC football championship until 1933 (before vacating for use of an ineligible player) under Coach Fred Thomsen. That year they went to their first bowl, the Dixie Classic in Dallas where they tied Centenary, 7-7. The Razorbacks claimed another SWC title in 1936 under Thomsen. They got to keep this one.

Coach John Barnhill ushered in the modern, post–World War II era at Arkansas when he won an SWC co-championship in 1946 and took the Razorbacks to their second and third bowls, including their first Cotton Bowl appearance. He also recruited the legendary Clyde Scott, an Olympic hurdler–running back. The 1954 Razorbacks won another SWC title under Coach Bowden Wyatt.

The glory years began when Frank Broyles arrived in 1958. Arkansas captured an SWC title in his second season. In five of seven seasons, from 1959 to 1965, Arkansas won or shared the SWC title and won a national title in 1964. Broyles took the Razorbacks to ten bowls and put them on the map nationally before he retired to the athletic director's post after the 1976 season. Lou Holtz and Ken Hatfield kept up the pace. Each took Arkansas to six straight bowls and competed at the top of the SWC.

Arkansas joined the Southeastern Conference in 1992, but during the last two decades the Razerbacks have failed to win an overall SEC title. They have claimed Western Division titles in 1995, 1998, 2002, and 2006. In 2010, they went to the Bowl Championship Series and lost to Ohio State in the Sugar Bowl. And in 2011, they finished with their highest ranking (fifth) since 1977 (third). Arkansas—including Bobby Petrino's replacement—has had six football coaches since 1990.

PROGRAM HIGHLIGHTS

NATIONAL CHAMPIONSHIPS (1): Arkansas claimed the 1964 FWAA and Helms national championships with an 11-0 record.

SWC CHAMPIONSHIPS (13): 1936, 1946, 1954, 1959, 1960, 1961, 1964, 1965, 1968, 1975, 1979, 1988, 1989

SEC CHAMPIONSHIPS (0): The Razorbacks joined the SEC in 1992 for football, the same year as South Carolina when the league expanded to twelve teams and split into divisions. Arkansas has won or tied for four division titles in 1995, 1998, 2002, and 2006, but has never won an SEC football championship game.

BOWL RECORD: 13-23-3 (36.1 percent). Last bowl—Arkansas beat Kansas State, 29-16, in the 2012 Cotton Bowl.

LONGEST WINNING STREAK: 22 games, 1963-66

WINNINGEST COACH: Ken Hatfield (1984-89), 55-17-1, 76.0 percent

HEISMAN TROPHY WINNERS OR HIGHEST HEISMAN FINISH: Darren McFadden, 2006 and 2007, runner-up each year

Frank Broyles

The Razorbacks coach posted a 70.8 percent winning percentage and took Arkansas to ten bowls during his nineteen seasons from 1958 to 1976. His 144 victories are 69 more than the nearest Razorback coach. His battles with Texas coach Darrell Royal, including the 1969 "Shootout" that determined the national title, rank among some of the best Razorback games of all time.

Loyd Phillips

The standout defensive tackle claimed the 1966 Outland Trophy, given to the best interior lineman in college football. Arkansas won the national championship his sophomore season, and Phillips never lost to Texas during his varsity career. During his three seasons, Arkansas compiled a 29-3 record.

Clyde "Smackover" Scott

Scott rushed for 1,463 yards from 1946 to 1948 and earned All-America honors his senior season when he averaged seven yards a carry. During his Razorback career, he became the first person from the school to win an Olympic medal when he earned a silver in the hurdles in 1948. His No. 12 was later retired.

Lance Alworth

This flanker was named to College and Pro Football Halls of Fame (San Diego Chargers and Dallas Cowboys). The slippery Alworth, who was born in Houston but grew up in Mississippi, was also college football's top punt returner in 1960 and 1961. Arkansas won or tied for the Southwest Conference title in each of his three seasons.

NOTABLE ALUMS

Pat Summerall—Famous pro football sportscaster

Jerry Jones and Jimmy Johnson—Oilman and owner of the Dallas Cowboys (Jones); Johnson was the team's head coach for two Super Bowl triumphs with Jones as owner; both played on the Razorbacks' only national football title team

J. William Fulbright—Former U.S. senator and U.S. representative who created the Fulbright Scholarship Program

Barry Switzer—University of Oklahoma football coach and later head coach of the Dallas Cowboys. He claimed one Super Bowl victory with Jerry Jones as owner

---

STADIUM

Donald W. Reynolds Stadium: The stadium, named after the Donrey Media benefactor, opened on September 24, 1938, when Arkansas defeated Oklahoma A&M, 27-7. The original stadium seated only 13,500. Over the years, because of various additions, the capacity rose to 50,000 seats prior to the 1985 season. In 2001, a 20,000-seat addition was completed and since then the capacity has hit 72,000, with overflow crowds on occasion. In 2007, the playing surface was dedicated as Frank Broyles Field, after its longtime athletic director and storied football coach.

FIGHT SONG

Hit that line! Hit that line! Keep on going.

Move the ball down the field!

Give a cheer. Rah! Rah! Never fear. Rah! Rah!

Arkansas will never yield!

On your toes, Razorbacks, to the finish,

Carry on with all your might!

For it's A-A-A-R-K-A-N-S-A-S for Arkansas!

Fight! Fight! Fi-i-i-ght!

MASCOTS

Tusk IV, a Russian boar that closely resembles the wild hog of football Coach Hugo Bezdek's era in the early 1900s, is the live Arkansas mascot. After a victory at LSU in 1909, Bezdek referred to his team as playing "like a wild band of Razorback hogs," a ferocious animal that occupied the state of Arkansas wooded countryside. Tusk IV is cared for by the Stokes family of Dardanelle, Arkansas, and travels to home games and special events.

In uniform (human mascots) are Big Red or the Fighting Razorback, Sue E (female hog), and Pork Chop (kid hog). Boss Hog is a nine-foot inflatable mascot.

MIZZOU CONNECTION

All-time football record vs. Missouri: 2-3

1906: Missouri 11, Arkansas 0 (Columbia)

1944: Arkansas 7, Missouri 6 (St. Louis)

1963: Missouri 7, Arkansas 6 (Little Rock)

2003: Arkansas 27, Missouri 14 (Independence Bowl, Shreveport, La.)

2008: Missouri 38, Arkansas 7 (Cotton Bowl, Dallas [2007 season])

In his only matchup against the man he replaced at Missouri, Dan Devine nipped Frank Broyles' Razorbacks in a hotly contested 1963 meeting. Incensed with the home-field chain gang at War Memorial Stadium, Devine moved the stakes when the officials denied the Tigers a first down, according to Bob Broeg's *Ol' Mizzou: A Century of Tiger Football*. It took six Arkansas state policemen to escort Devine back to the bench. Oddly, it was the final regular-season matchup between two schools situated just three hundred miles apart. Under Gary Pinkel, the Tigers fell to Arkansas in their first of three Independence Bowl appearances but avenged the loss four years later in a one-sided Cotton Bowl clash. Snubbed out of a BCS bowl, the Tigers earned their school-record twelfth victory behind Tony Temple's 281 rushing yards and four touchdowns, both Cotton Bowl records.

On second thought: Midway through his fifth season as Missouri's men's basketball coach, Mike Anderson dismissed rumors that he wanted the head-coaching job at Arkansas, where he was Nolan Richardson's right-hand man for seventeen years. "I plan on being at Missouri for a long time, retire here," he told the *Columbia Daily Tribune* on March 4, 2011. "I'm happy." Three weeks later, he was even happier as the new head coach at Arkansas. Anderson wasn't the first head coach to make the move from Tiger to Razorback. Broyles stunned Missouri after the 1957 football season, his lone year on the MU sideline, when he left for Arkansas, where he won seven Southwest Conference titles and served as UA's longtime athletic director.

All in the family: The athletic departments at both schools owe a lot to the Walton family. Raised in Columbia, Missouri, the Walton brothers, Sam and Bud, ran a series of variety stores in both states and in 1962 launched what is now known as Wal-Mart in Rogers, Arkansas. Years later, Bud paid for half the $30 million construction of Arkansas' basketball arena, which bears his name. Missouri's track and soccer stadium bears the name of Bud's wife, Audrey Walton. Bud's daughters Ann Walton Kroenke and Nancy Walton Laurie and their families have also been major benefactors at Missouri. The Laurie family paid for one third of MU's $75 million Mizzou Arena, which was initially named Paige Sports Arena after their daughter.

GAME DAY

MEDIA

Broadcasting the Game: KABZ-FM 103.7 in Little Rock, and KUOA-AM 1290 and KUOA-FM 105.3 in Fayetteville

Covering the Razorbacks: www.arkansasonline.com/news/sports (*Arkansas Democrat-Gazette*), www.nwaonline.com/sports (*Northwest Arkansas Newspapers*)

TAILGATING

General Parking/Tailgating on War Memorial Golf Course is a longstanding tradition for Razorback football games. General Parking/Tailgating is available on a first-come basis, and fans pay the $20 fee when they arrive. There are no trailers allowed in the general tailgating area. Entrances into the General Parking/Tailgating section are available in two locations. Fans can enter off Interstate 630 onto Fair Park heading north and turn onto Clubhouse Drive. Or, fans can enter from Markham to Taylor Street.

The reserved tailgating area opens at 6 a.m. on game days. The tailgating space is designed to accommodate one vehicle and a 10' x 10' tent directly behind or in front of the vehicle. The reserved tailgating area closes to motor traffic at 10:30 a.m. The golf course closes two hours after the game. Vehicles remaining are towed at owner's expense.

SHUTTLE

Free off-campus public parking is available off of Razorback Road one mile south of the stadium between Martin Luther King (6th Street) and 15th Street. Shuttle service is provided starting four hours before kickoff and runs continuously after the game.

TRADITIONS

Calling the Hogs: The Hog Call began when a group of farmers used it to cheer on the team in the 1920s. Now thousands of Razorback fans make it ritual at all athletic contests in which Arkansas participates. Fans begin with their hands raised high with the "Wooooooo"; then go down with "Pig!"; and then back up with "Sooie!"

Wooooooo, Pig! Sooie!
Wooooooo, Pig! Sooie!
Wooooooo, Pig! Sooie!
RAZORBACKS!

Senior Walk: Starting in 1905, Arkansas graduates wrote their names in the wet cement of a campus sidewalk. Later graduating classes had their names engraved in the sidewalk. And in the 1930s, classes graduating prior to 1904 had their names added. An invention developed in 1986, the "Sand Hog" was designed by the school's physical plant specifically for inscribing names in Senior Walk. Names on Senior Walk stretch over three miles on campus.

B-BALL, ETC.

The Razorbacks won the NCAA Division I Men's Basketball championship in 1994 under Coach Nolan Richardson and advanced to the NCAA title game again in 1995 before losing to UCLA. In all, Arkansas has made six Final Fours, but none in the last seventeen years. Mike Anderson, an assistant under Richardson during the glory years, is now the Razorbacks' head coach and is trying to rebuild the program that has tailed off in the years since Richardson departed. Arkansas is known as a track power. The Razorbacks won forty-two NCAA team championships in indoor and outdoor and cross-country under John McConnell during a thirty-six-year period from 1972 to 2008.

WOOOOOOO PIG SOOIE!

ABOUT TOWN

Fayetteville is located on the outskirts of the Boston Mountains, part of the Ozarks, and is the third-largest city in Arkansas. Originally named Washington after President George, it was later named after General Lafayette, a French general who helped America gain freedom in the Revolutionary War, and was incorporated in 1836. The hilly area is considered a great place to work, play, and retire and has stunning foliage during football season. Wal-Mart is based in nearby Bentonville, and its success affects the Fayetteville economy. It is one of four Fortune 500 Companies based in Arkansas. Tyson Foods, based in adjacent Springdale, is another.

LODGING

In Northwest Arkansas, the chain hotel rooms fill up quickly. But here are three that present something different.

Inn at the Mill: Just five miles from Fayetteville, the hotel is actually a nineteenth-century water-powered grain mill that has been transformed into sleeping rooms and restaurant. It is located in the foothills of the Ozarks near Interstate 540 between Springdale and Fayetteville. In the past, hotel guests have enjoyed some nice touches such as wine and cheese in the afternoons. It has all the amenities of a regular hotel. *3906 Greathouse Springs Rd., Johnson, AR 72741, 479-443-1800*

Inn at Carnall Hall: Built in 1905 in memory of Miss Ella Howison Carnall, this was the first women's residence hall on the Arkansas campus. In renovating the dorm, every one of the fifty rooms is unique. Ella's Restaurant offers a free continental breakfast. A bar is located in the hotel. *465 N. Arkansas Ave., Fayetteville, AR 72701, 479-582-0400, 800-295-9118, www.innatcarnallhall.com*

Another good source for hotels is in Fayetteville is www.fayettevillear.com/HotelsMotels.

Pratt Place Inn: There are only seven accommodations in this boutique hotel, which is considered the best in Fayetteville. Complimentary breakfast is served wherever you wish: in bed, on the veranda, or in the dining room. Afternoon refreshments are available in the parlor. The inn combines Southern charm with European elegance in a secluded 140 acres of pasture and woodland near Razorback Stadium. Must call to get rates. *2231 West Markham Rd., Fayetteville, AR 72712, 479-966-4441, www.prattplaceinn.com*

EATING

Herman's Ribhouse: Hole in the wall that you could miss because it looks like a deserted building. Open since 1964. President Bill Clinton appears on the website. Besides the ribs, steaks, garlic chicken, and seafood are excellent. Love those hash browns and Texas Toast. Shrimp Remoulade is a specialty. *2901 N. College Ave., Fayetteville, AR 72703, 479-442-9671, www.hermansribhouse.com*

Bordinos: Fine Northern Italian food in Northwest Arkansas? Find it here. A nice wine list. Make it a date in a romantic setting before or after the game. A couple of items catch the eye: Venetian Style Beef Ragù Lasagna (Spinach, Mozzarella, Spicy Tomato Sauce) and Arkansas Arborio Risotto (Shrimp, Leek, Pumpkin). *310 W. Dickson St., Fayetteville, AR 72701, 479-527-6795, www. bordinos.com*

Hugo's: Just off the square . . . in the basement. Now being operated in its thirty-fifth year. Nice selection of beers and wines. A few entrees, but mostly sandwiches and appetizers. Burgers and homemade fries are a highlight of the menu that ranges from crepes to nachos. Famous for beer cheese soup on chilly autumn afternoons or evenings. *25 ½ N. Block Ave., Fayetteville, AR 72701, 479-521-7585, www.hugosfayetteville.com*

SIGHTSEEING

Clinton House Museum: Only an 1,800-square-foot house, but it is where Bill married Hillary seventeen years before he became president of the United States. Rarely seen memorabilia from early in his political career are displayed. *930 W. Clinton Dr., Fayetteville, AR 72701. Hours: 8:30 a.m. to 4:30 p.m. (M-Sat.). Tickets $5. 479-444-0066 or 877-245-6445 www.clintonhousemuseum.org*

Arkansas Air Museum: The history of Arkansas aviation is displayed from racing planes in the 1920s and 1930s through the jet age. Many of the planes can still fly. The all-wood white hangar is a former headquarters for an aviator training post during World War II. *4290 South School Ave., Fayetteville, AR 72701. Hours: 11 a.m. to 4:30 p.m. (M-F, Sun.); 10 a.m. to 4:30 p.m. (Sat.). Tickets $8 adults. $4 children (6-12), 479-521-4947, www.arkairmuseum.org*

SHOPPING

Northwest Arkansas Mall: American Eagle, Banana Republic, Bath & Body Works, The Buckle, Candy Craze, Choices, Christopher & Banks, Dillard's, Eddie Bauer, Express, Finish Line, Forever21, Gymboree, JC Penney, Lane Bryant, Lenscrafters, Masons, Maurices, New York & Company, Pacific Sunwear, Payless Shoes, Rack Room Shoes, Razorback Shop, Romancing the Stone, Sears, Sunglass Hut, Things Remembered, Tradehome Shoes, Victoria's Secret, Warren's Shoes. *4201 North Shiloh Dr., Fayetteville, AR 72703, Hours: 10 a.m.-9 p.m. (M-Sat.) noon-6 p.m. (Sun.), 479-521-6151, www.northwestarkansasmall.com*

Hog Heaven: No matter if it is game day or not, the store is open most days, inside the Razorbacks' hoops home. Everything from the famous Razorback Lids to polka dot dog collars. *1270 Leroy Pond Rd., Fayetteville, AR 72701 (Bud Walton Arena), 479-575-3815*

NIGHTLIFE

21st Amendment Bar and Lounge: One of the spots on Dickson Street where all the activity moves as the night goes on. Largest selection of liquor in Fayetteville. Reservations often needed for Friday and Saturday nights. *406 W. Dickson St., Fayetteville, AR 72701, 479-856-6686, www.21stamendmentbar.com*

The Common Grounds Gourmet Espresso Bar & Restaurant: Open from 7 a.m. until midnight every day. Varied groups seen here: the early morning coffee and muffin crowd; those who choose a leisurely lunch to the after-dinner-drink scene. Full bar and great dessert menu. Live music schedule. *412 W. Dickson St., Fayetteville, AR 72701, 479-442-3515, www.commongroundsar.com*

TRAVELING TO FAYETTEVILLE?

It's the shortest trip in the SEC for Missouri, just a 300-mile drive from Columbia—or about 350 from St. Louis and 250 from the Kansas City area. The Mizzou Alumni Association hosts a Tiger Tailgate. Visit MizzouSportsTravel.com for more information on tickets and pricing.

AUBURN

Imagine the 2010 BCS national championship trophy being awarded to East Alabama Male College.

Or

"The winner of the 2010 Heisman Trophy is . . . quarterback Cam Newton of the Agricultural and Mechanical College of Alabama."

Or

"Let's go down to the sideline to speak with the winning coach, Gene Chizik of Alabama Polytechnic Institute."

Those are three names that Auburn University was known by before it officially became Auburn University in 1960, three years after the school won its first national football championship.

The school opened in 1859, twenty years after the town was incorporated in February 1839 covering just two square miles. Because of the Civil War, in 1861 the school closed almost as soon as it opened and didn't re-open until 1866. It floundered financially until the Morrill Act in 1872 made the school the first land-grant institution in the South.

AUBURN UNIVERSITY

Students: 25,649

Auburn: pop. 53,380

Jordan-Hare Stadium: seats 87,451

Colors: Burnt Orange and Navy Blue

Nickname: Tigers

Mascot: Aubie

Campus Attractions: Toomer's Corner, Jule Collins Smith Museum

Phone: 334-844-4000 (general information)
334-844-8888 (campus police)
334-844-4750 (athletic department)

Tickets: 334-844-4040 or aubtix.com

For the next one hundred years, the school and the town of Auburn rode an economic rollercoaster. But what really gave the town, the university, and the football program a boost came in 1957 when Interstate 85 began construction. Suddenly, Auburn was not a remote outpost anymore, and no one could have been happier than Tigers' football coach Ralph "Shug" Jordan. He suddenly had two things to sell to recruits—easier access to the campus and a fuller stadium, because fans now could get to Auburn more easily.

Jordan, an Auburn graduate, had been head coach for seven years when his 1957 team won the Associated Press national championship. The Tigers went 10-0, including 7-0 in the SEC, outscoring opponents 207-28 with six shutouts, the last of which was a season-ending 40-0 whitewash of the University of Alabama.

That defeat was the last straw for Alabama, which promptly went out and hired a guy named Bear Bryant. Once Bryant arrived, Jordan never again won an SEC championship. But the Tigers still had some excellent teams under Jordan—six of the twenty-five squads he coached from 1951 to 1975 finished the season ranked in the top ten.

After a lull for most of the 1960s in which Jordan's teams never won more than six games, his program roared back to prominence from 1969 to 1971 thanks to quarterback Pat Sullivan and wide receiver Terry Beasley, one of the best pass-catch duos in SEC history. Sullivan won the 1971 Heisman Trophy, which didn't happen again for Auburn until 1985 when running back Vincent "Bo" Jackson rumbled for 1,786 yards and 17 touchdowns.

By the time Jackson was terrorizing defenses, Auburn had re-established itself among the national powers. Pat Dye, a former Bear Bryant assistant hired by AU in 1981, won four SEC championships in his twelve seasons. While Terry Bowden, Dye's successor, saw his first Auburn team go unbeaten at 11-0, the Tigers were on NCAA probation and ineligible for postseason play. The 2004

PROGRAM HIGHLIGHTS

NATIONAL CHAMPIONSHIPS (2): 1957, 2010

SEC CHAMPIONSHIPS (7): 1957, 1983, 1987, 1988, 1989, 2004, 2010

BOWL RECORD: 22-13-2 (.608). Last bowl—42-23 over Virginia in 2011 Chick-fil-A Bowl

LONGEST WINNING STREAK: 20 games (twice), 1956-58

WINNINGEST COACH: Ralph "Shug" Jordan (1951-75), 176-83-6, 67.5 percent

HEISMAN TROPHY WINNERS OR HIGHEST HEISMAN FINISH: Quarterback Pat Sullivan, 1971 winner; running back Bo Jackson, 1985 winner; quarterback Cam Newton, 2010 winner

Tigers of Tommy Tuberville were also a perfect 13-0 and finished second nationally, but they didn't qualify to play in the BCS national championship game.

A BCS title game finally materialized in 2010 when a junior college transfer named Cam Newton stepped in at quarterback, won the Heisman Trophy, and guided Auburn to a 14-0 record and a three-point victory over Oregon in the BCS national championship game.

Fifty-three seasons and five coaches after AU's first national title under Jordan, Auburn had something to gloat over its in-state rival Alabama.

LEGENDS

Ralph "Shug" Jordan

The Auburn coach won 176 games in 25 years, including a national title in 1957. He also produced twenty All-Americans and a Heisman Trophy winner.

Pat Sullivan

The AU quarterback won the 1971 Heisman Trophy by 152 points over Cornell running back Ed Marinaro. Sullivan has been a college coach most of his life and is currently the head coach at Samford University in his hometown of Birmingham.

Vincent "Bo" Jackson

His 1985 Heisman Trophy selection was the start of his national notoriety. Originally bypassing the NFL to play Major League Baseball for the Kansas City Royals, he later played football for the NFL's Los Angeles Raiders. Jackson became a pop culture icon thanks to a Nike shoe campaign called "Bo Knows," which promoted the company's cross-training shoes.

Cam Newton

The junior college transfer started his college career at Florida as backup quarterback in 2007 to Heisman Trophy–winning quarterback Tim Tebow. Newton captured the whole shooting match in 2010, guiding AU to the national championship while winning the Heisman and breaking Tebow's single-season SEC total offense record.

NOTABLE ALUMS

Jimmy Buffett—Singer, author, beachbum extraordinaire

John Heisman—Namesake of the Heisman Trophy who was a former college football, basketball, and baseball coach

Dr. Kathryn Thornton—Space shuttle astronaut and second woman in space

Jimmy Johnson—Cartoonist of comic strip *Arlo and Janis*

STADIUM

Jordan-Hare: Since opening in 1929 with 7,500 seats, the stadium now seats a hefty 87,451 fans. It was named Cliff Hare Stadium in 1949 to honor Clifford Leroy Hare, a member of Auburn's first football team, then re-named Jordan-Hare in 1973 to honor AU coach Ralph "Shug" Jordan, who was still coaching the Tigers.

MASCOTS

A mascot that started out as a cartoon character in 1959 on the cover of an Auburn home-game program, Aubie—Auburn's costumed Tiger mascot— has become one of the most animated and award-winning mascots in all of college sports. He made the transition from being a cartoon to a sideline mascot in 1979, when he debuted at the SEC basketball tournament. Three to four Auburn students each year usually wear the Aubie outfit and infuse it with the personality that has resulted in Aubie being selected seven times by the Universal Cheerleaders Association's No. 1 collegiate mascot in the nation. Aubie's most recent national title came in January 2012.

FIGHT SONG

"WAR EAGLE"

War . . . Eagle, fly down the field, Ever to conquer, never to yield.

War . . . Eagle fearless and true. Fight on, you orange and blue

Go! Go! Go!

On to vic'try, strike up the band,

Give 'em hell, give 'em hell.

Stand up and yell, Hey! War . . . Eagle, win for Auburn,

Power of Dixie Land!

MIZZOU CONNECTION

Courtesy Mizzou Athletics Media Relations

All-time football record vs. Missouri: 0-1

1973: Missouri 34, Auburn 17 (Sun Bowl; El Paso, Texas)

The Tigers of Auburn and Missouri have clashed just once, but the cats from Auburn hardly bared their claws in the only meeting, the 1973 Sun Bowl. Auburn survived an early onslaught in El Paso, Texas, and sliced its deficit to 21-10 with a touchdown pass in the closing seconds of the first half. One problem: The Tigers—the ones from Auburn—left eight seconds on the clock. Oops. Just beaten on the seventeen-yard TD, Mizzou cornerback John Moseley had the last laugh, returning the ensuing kickoff eighty-four yards for a touchdown. Ball game.

Familiar felines: More than a dozen Division I athletic programs share the Tiger nickname, and Auburn and Missouri have two of the most animated Tiger mascots in college sports. Auburn's Aubie began appearing at Tiger games in 1979 and is a seven-time winner of his trade's top honor: Collegiate Mascot of the Year, awarded each year by the Universal Cheerleaders Association. Missouri's Truman the Tiger—named after thirty-third president and Missouri native Harry Truman—came to life in 1986 and has twice been named the country's best mascot, by the Universal Cheerleaders Association in 1990 and the National Cheerleading Association in 2004.

On the prowl: In the 1960s, Auburn began a game-day ritual that others schools have since borrowed over the years, including Missouri. Former Auburn athletic director David Housel once called Tiger Walk "the most copied tradition in all of college football." A couple hours before kickoff, Tiger Walk gets started as Auburn players and coaches ceremoniously walk down Donahue Drive to Jordan-Hare Stadium. They are greeted by thousands of fans lining the street. Gary Pinkel adopted a similar custom at Missouri in recent years as players and coaches make Tiger Walk—catchy, isn't it?—across a pedestrian bridge over Providence Road and through the Memorial Stadium parking lots, where they are feted by fans before the game.

GAME DAY

MEDIA

Broadcasting the Game: WKKR-FM 97.7 in Auburn-Opelika, along with WAPI-FM 100.5 and WAPI-AM 1070 in Birmingham

Covering the Tigers: www.al.com/auburnfootball (*Birmingham News, Mobile Register*), www2.oanow.com/sports/college/auburn (*Opelika-Auburn News*), www.AuburnUndercover.com

TAILGATING

Tailgates can't be set up on campus until 4 p.m. the day before a home game. You can't use any university utilities, you can't tailgate and grill on parking decks, and you can't place your grill within fifty feet of campus buildings or in other designated no-grill areas. The origin of that last rule came after a tailgater at the 1996 Auburn-LSU game had his grill too close to Auburn's old basketball arena, known as "The Barn." While Mr. Careless Tailgater was in Jordan-Hare watching LSU beat Auburn 19-15, ashes from the grill ignited a fire that burned the arena to the ground. ESPN cameras showed flames shooting as high as Jordan-Hare's east-side upper deck. So follow the rules and don't burn down anything.

SHUTTLE

There are numerous free shuttles, thanks to Tiger Transit, that run from off-campus and on-campus stops. Off-campus stops include Village Mall (*1627-53 Opelika Rd.*), Auburn University Regional Airport (fly-ins only), Sam's Club (*2335 Bent Creek Rd., exit 57*), Duck Samford Park (*333 Airport Rd., exit 57*), and Auburn City Softball Complex (*2560 S. College, exit 51*). The main on-campus pick-up and drop-off spot is War Eagle Way. You can track the progress of your bus on your smart phone by visiting the Tiger Transit website at www.auburn.edu/transit and clicking the "Find Your Bus" link.

TRADITIONS

War Eagle: It's not only Auburn's battle cry, it's a greeting between Auburn fans and alums. Instead of saying, "Hello," they say, "War Eagle." The origination of "War Eagle" stems from the first Georgia-Auburn game in 1892 played at Atlanta's Piedmont Park. An Auburn faculty member sat in the stands with an eagle he had raised since he served in the Civil War. During the game, the eagle suddenly took off and began soaring above the crowd as Auburn mounted a touchdown drive. Auburn fans and students began screaming "War Eagle" as their team recorded a 10-0 win. Victory in hand, at the game's end, the eagle suddenly dived, crashed into the ground, and died.

Tiger Walk: It seems like every school in the South has the pregame ritual where their team walks in street clothes through a corridor of adoring fans as they enter their stadium dressing room to prepare for battle. Well, all those teams copied Auburn, because the Tigers did it first back in the early 1960s, walking several hundred yards from Sewell Hall, which at one time was primarily the athletic dorm, to Jordan-Hare. The largest crowd ever for a Tiger Walk, estimated at 20,000, was before the 1989 Alabama game, which was the first time the Crimson Tide had ever played at Auburn. Until then, all Alabama-Auburn games had traditionally been played in Birmingham's Legion Field.

B-BALL, ETC.

Yes, Auburn is the school that gave the world Charles Barkley, Naismith Basketball Hall of Famer, outrageous NBA analyst, and Weight Watchers guru. But for a school that is several hours from a beach, Auburn has a swimming program beyond belief. The Tigers have won thirteen NCAA swimming and diving national championships, eight men's titles and five women's. In February 2012, the Auburn men won their sixteenth straight SEC swimming and diving championship. There is always a load of Auburn swimmers competing in the Olympics, like in the 2008 Beijing Games where five Auburn swimmers won thirteen medals.

ABOUT TOWN

Poet Oliver Goldsmith's 1770 poem, "The Deserted Village" gave the town of Auburn an identity. One line from the poem reads, "Sweet Auburn, loveliest village on the plain," and the town is still viewed that way. Downtown Auburn still has that basic Mayberry feel to it, with Toomer's Drugs and its exquisite lemonade. There is more urban sprawl on South College Street that connects the campus and downtown with Interstate 85, which runs southwest to Montgomery and northeast to Atlanta. And that's okay, because even with Auburn sprouting to almost 54,000 residents, it has still maintained its quaint downtown area full of shops and eateries.

LODGING

The Hotel at Auburn University and Dixon Conference Center: This hotel is the best of both worlds—an ultra-modern hotel with comfort, class, and golf privileges at the private Auburn University Golf Club and the convenient location of being within walking distance of the university and downtown shops and nightlife. *241 South College St., Auburn, AL 36830, 334-821-8200 or 800-228-2876, www.auhcc.com*

Auburn Marriott Opelika Hotel & Conference Center at Grand National: If you check in to this place without your golf clubs, you should be arrested. This slice of heaven is just ten minutes from Auburn's campus. Most of its 114 rooms and 15 suites overlook a beautiful lake and a 54-hole course designed by renowned architect Robert Trent Jones. *3700 Robert Trent Jones Trail, Opelika, AL 36801, 334-741-9292 or 800-593-6456, www.marriott.com/hotels/travel/csgab-auburn-marriott-opelika-hotel-and-conference-center-at-grand-national/*

Most of the hotels in the Auburn area are in Opelika, which melds into Auburn from the east. You can also fly into Atlanta, rent a car, and drive one hundred miles southwest on Interstate 85 to Auburn.

EATING

Hamilton's on Magnolia: This warm, inviting downtown spot is perfect for dining on the patio when the weather is just right. The best deal is a $9 express lunch special where you choose a soup, a salad, and a wrap. *174 E. Magnolia Ave., Auburn, AL 36830, 334-887-2677, www.hamiltonsonmagnolia.com*

Amsterdam Café: Do you start off with grilled shrimp and grits (yes, it's a crazy combo but that's how we roll in the South) or advance directly to the Gulf red snapper served with crawfish dirty rice? *410 S. Gay St., Auburn, AL 36830, 334-826-8181, www.amsterdamcafeauburn.com*

Niffer's Place: Founded and owned since 1991 by former Auburn swimmer Keely Beasecker, there's a homemade taste to just about everything on the menu. Prices are family-friendly and the portions are generous, so bring a skinny wallet and a huge appetite. *1151 Opelika Rd., Auburn, AL 36830, 334-821-3118, www.niffersplace.com*

SIGHTSEEING

Toomer's Corner: This is the intersection of Magnolia and College Avenue where downtown Auburn ends and the Auburn University campus begins. It's named for former Alabama state senator Sheldon Toomer, who founded Toomer's Drugs in 1896 on the northeast corner of the Magnolia and College intersection. Toomer's Drugs is still there, just across the street from two massive oak trees that are wrapped in toilet paper by celebrating fans every time Auburn wins a football game.

Chewacla State Park: This gorgeous 696-acre park features a twenty-six-acre lake and has something for everybody that loves the outdoors—fishing, swimming, hiking, boating. There are cabins available for rentals and a modern campground. *124 Shell Toomer Parkway, Auburn, AL 36830, 334-887-5621, www.alapark.com/Chewacla/*

SHOPPING

Tiger Town: A collection of fifty-three shops and restaurants—most of the chain variety you know by heart—is located on 132 acres on the corner of Interstate 85 and Highway 280 in Opelika. *Tiger Town Parkway, Opelika, AL 36804*

Toomer's Drugs: The old-fashioned soda fountain is the attraction. And even if you think all lemonade in the world tastes the same, once you've had a Toomer's special formula lemonade (go for the thirty-two-ounce $3.75 glass), you'll realize you'd crawl across the Sahara Desert to drink this stuff. *100 N. College St., Auburn, AL 36830, 334-887-3488, www.toomersdrugs.com*

NIGHTLIFE

War Eagle Supper Club: The fact that *Playboy Magazine* rated this joint as one of the nation's fifty best college bars is reason enough to check it out. It even has a bar serving just shots that's on a broken-down school bus on the back deck. *2061 S. College St., Auburn, AL 36830, 334-821-4455, www. wareaglesupperclub.com*

Bourbon Street Bar: A three-floor bar with a level for every taste. The ground floor features live music, floor two is for pool and darts, and floor three has a rooftop patio where you can kick it at a slow pace. *103 N. College St., Auburn, AL 36830, 334-887-1166*

Skybar Café: Live bands and ridiculously inexpensive drink specials ($2 tallboys all night on Tuesdays and Thursdays) keep this downtown Auburn hangout a-hoppin'. *136 W. Magnolia Ave., Auburn, AL 36830, 334-821-4001, www. auskybar.com*

TRAVELING TO AUBURN?

It's a 115-mile drive to Auburn's campus from the nearest major airport, Birmingham-Shuttlesworth International, which offers nonstop flights to St. Louis and Kansas City. Columbia Regional Airport offers regular service through Memphis International, where you can pick up a connection to Birmingham. Montgomery Regional Airport is only sixty miles from Auburn but only connects to Atlanta, Charlotte, and Dallas. Otherwise, Auburn is a lengthy drive from Missouri—610 miles from St. Louis, 730 from Columbia, and 860 from Kansas City. The Mizzou Alumni Association hosts a Tiger Tailgate. Visit MizzouSportsTravel.com for more information on tickets and pricing.

FLORIDA

In 1853 the state-funded East Florida Seminary took over the Kingsbury Academy in Ocala. The seminary moved to Gainesville in the 1860s and later was consolidated with the state's land-grant Florida Agricultural College in Lake City. In 1905, by state legislative action, the college became a university and was moved to Gainesville. Classes first met with 102 students on the present site on September 26, 1906. The University of Florida officially opened its doors to women in 1947 and eleven years later to African-American students.

The Gator football program got its start in 1906 under Coach James Forsythe and played its games at the city ballpark through 1911, before moving to on-campus Fleming Field from 1912 to 1929. The Gators set up shop in their current stadium in 1930, albeit it was much smaller then.

UNIVERSITY OF FLORIDA

Students: 52,122

Gainesville: pop. 124,354

Ben Hill Griffin Stadium: seats 88,548

Colors: Orange and Blue

Nickname: Gators

Mascot: Albert and Alberta

Campus Attractions: Century Tower, Museum of Natural History

Phone: 352-392-3261 (general information)
352-392-1111 (campus police)
352-375-4683 (athletic department)

Tickets: 352-375-4683, ext. 6800 or www.GatorZone.com/tickets

Florida started competing in the Southeastern Conference in 1933 but didn't win its first league football title (that it got to keep or was eligible for) until 1991 under Coach Steve Spurrier. But Florida football still was noteworthy, and it started to generate some momentum in the early 1960s under Coach Ray Graves. Spurrier, a Heisman Trophy–winning quarterback for the Gators, led UF to the 1966 Sugar Bowl (1965 season) and the Orange Bowl the following season.

In the early and mid-1980s, Coach Charley Pell established the Gators as a national power, but an NCAA probation ended his reign. It took Spurrier's arrival in 1990 to get things rolling again. His teams dominated the SEC in the 1990s and won a national championship in 1996 behind quarterback Danny Wuerffel. Coach Urban Meyer won a couple more SEC and national titles, in 2006 and 2008.

Since 1985, Florida has been a member of the Association of American Universities, a higher-education organization of the top sixty-three public and private institutions in North America.

PROGRAM HIGHLIGHTS

NATIONAL CHAMPIONSHIPS (3): 1996, 2006, 2008

SEC CHAMPIONSHIPS (8): 1991, 1993, 1994, 1995, 1996, 2000, 2006, 2008 (Florida had to vacate the 1984 SEC title and was ineligible for titles in 1985 and 1991 when on the field it tied for the title in 1985 and had the best SEC record in 1990).

BOWL RECORD: 20-19 (51.3 percent). Last bowl—24-17 win over Ohio State in the 2012 Gator Bowl

LONGEST WINNING STREAK: 22 games (2008-2009)

WINNINGEST COACH: Steve Spurrier (1990-2001), 122-27-1, 81.7 percent

HEISMAN TROPHY WINNERS OR HIGHEST HEISMAN FINISH: Quarterback Steve Spurrier, 1966 winner; Quarterback Danny Wuerffel, 1996 winner; Quarterback Tim Tebow, 2007 winner

Tim Tebow

Brilliant as a sophomore, Tebow became the first of that class to sweep Heisman Trophy, Davey O'Brien, and Maxwell awards. As a junior in 2008, Tebow led the Gators to their third national football title and was named the game's MVP in the Gators' victory over Oklahoma.

Emmitt Smith

Much-decorated running back who became the NFL's all-time leading rusher in 2002, Smith was a part of three Super Bowl–winning teams as a member of the Dallas Cowboys. As a Gator, he gained nearly four thousand yards on the ground from 1987 to 1989. He is a member of both the College Football and Pro Football Halls of Fame.

Jack Youngblood

Defensive end who is a member of both the College Football and Pro Football Halls of Fame, Youngblood is considered by some to be the best at his position in Gator history. He was named to the *Gainesville Sun*'s Florida Team of the Century in 1999. After his college career from 1968 to 1970, he was a five-time All-Pro for the Los Angeles Rams.

Wilber Marshall

A two-time consensus All-American at outside linebacker, Marshall had 58 tackles for loss and 343 tackles (210 unassisted) during his career from 1980 to 1983. He has been inducted into the College Football Hall of Fame. After his college career he played for the Chicago Bears and Washington Redskins and was an All-Pro three times.

NOTABLE ALUMS

Bob Graham—Former United States senator and Florida governor

Frank Shorter—Olympic Gold Medalist

Faye Dunaway—Actress

Erin Andrews—ESPN sideline reporter

STADIUM

Ben Hill Griffin: The stadium opened in 1930 with 21,769 seats—the first thirty-two rows on the west, east, and north sides of the current stadium. The stadium was dedicated on November 8, 1930, when Florida lost to Alabama, 20-0, and the legendary Red Barber, a Florida student, had the play-by-play call. Numerous facelifts and seating additions have boosted Florida's capacity to 88,548, with home crowds going over 90,000. In 1991, Coach Steve Spurrier nicknamed the stadium "The Swamp" because he said: "The Swamp is where Gators live. We feel comfortable there, but we hope our opponents feel tentative. A swamp is hot and sticky and can be dangerous."

FIGHT SONG

"THE ORANGE AND BLUE"

On, brave old Flor-i-da, just keep on marching on your way!

Oh, brave old Flor-i-da, and we will cheer you on your play!

Rah! Rah! Rah!

And as you march a-long, we'll sing your victory song anew

With all of your might Go on and Fight Gators

Fight for Dixie's rightly proud of you

So give a cheer for the Orange and Blue

Waving for-ev-er, forever

Pride of old Flor-i-da, May she droop nev-er

We'll sing a song for the flag to-day. Cheer for the team at play!

On to the goal we'll fight our way for Flor-i-da.

MASCOT

In the early 1900s, the Gator was adopted as the University of Florida mascot when it was chosen for a pennant because it was a creature native to the state. A merchant visited his son in Charlottesville, Virginia, and discovered Florida had no mascot after looking at pennants for the Yale Bulldogs and Princeton Tigers. He decided it needed one.

The first live alligator, Albert, came to the school in 1957. Several different live alligators assumed the role of Albert over the years, and even a robotic, motorized reptile held the role. It wasn't until 1970 that Albert became personified on the field as a full-body vinyl costume. Alberta the Alligator was introduced in 1986 as Albert's sidekick and friend.

MIZZOU CONNECTION

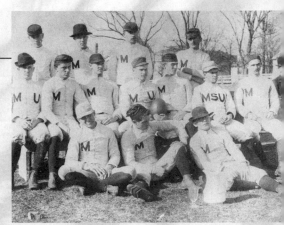

All-time football record vs. Missouri: 0-1

1966: Missouri 20, Florida 18 (Sugar Bowl, New Orleans)

A year before he would win the Heisman Trophy, Gators quarterback Steve Spurrier set Sugar Bowl records for pass attempts (45), completions (27), and passing yards (352)—and it still wasn't enough against Dan Devine's ferocious Tigers. In the thirty-three-year history of the Sugar Bowl, Spurrier became the first MVP to come from the losing team, only because Missouri needed a collective

Courtesy Mizzou Athletics Media Relations

effort to overcome the prolific passer. Behind halfback Charlie Brown and QB Gary Lane, the Tigers outgained Florida 257 to -2 in rushing yards, while the MU defense thwarted three fourth-quarter two-point conversions, all Spurrier pass attempts. "We have never hit a quarterback so often or so hard, but he hung in there to do a great job," Tigers defensive coordinator Al Onofrio told the *Columbia Daily Tribune* after the win.

Training ground: A handful of coaches have worked at both Florida and Missouri—Frank Broyles, Bill Cubit, Jon Hoke, and Ricky Hunley—but both programs have especially proven to produce NFL coaching careers. Among the league's head coaches at the start of 2012, two played at Florida, Buffalo's Chan Gailey and Jacksonville's Mike Mularkey, while Washington's Mike Shanahan was a Gator assistant in the early 1980s. Past Missouri assistants have gone to the NFL, too, most notably Philadelphia head coach Andy Reid. Other 2012 NFL assistants with Missouri years on their résumés include Marty Mornhinweg (Eagles), Dave Toub (Bears), Matt Eberflus (Cowboys), Dave McGinnis (Rams), Andy Moeller (Ravens), Dirk Koetter (Falcons), and Ken Flajole (Saints).

On the big screen: Missouri alumni include several Oscar-nominated actors—Robert Loggia, Tom Berenger, Chris Cooper, and Brad Pitt. The most decorated star from Mizzou might be George C. Scott, whose film career includes his signature title role in the 1970 classic *Patton*. Three years later, he shared the silver screen with Hollywood's most famous alum from the University of Florida, Faye Dunaway, in *Oklahoma Crude*, a critically acclaimed Western set during the Oklahoma oil boom.

GAME DAY

MEDIA

Broadcasting the Game: WRUF-FM 103.7, WRUF-AM 850 in Gainesville, along with WFXJ-AM 930 in Jacksonville

Covering the Gators: www.gainesville.com/section/sports (*Gainesville Sun*), www.orlandosentinel.com/sports (*Orlando Sentinel*)

TAILGATING

Free first-come, first-serve RV parking is located on Hull Road west of SW 34th Street behind the Hilton Hotel and Conference Center. Once you enter the parking area the road will fork and the free RV parking is to the left (south portion of the lot). The lot opens at 6 p.m. on Friday night and is open until Sunday at noon. The only exception is the Homecoming weekend when the lot opens on Thursday at 6 p.m.

You may tailgate within your spot (in front or behind your vehicle) or in any open grass area. Please take special care to not block the road and/or walkways. Music must be confined to your tailgate area. Tents may not be used within a parking spot. Golf carts, mopeds and scooters will not be allowed in parking lots and surrounding streets on game day.

SHUTTLE

Utilize the RTS Shuttle Service to avoid the limited parking on campus on game days from the Oaks Mall, Hilton University of Florida Conference Center, the Village Center in Haile Plantation, Tioga Town Center, Downtown Parking Garage, and Garage IX (ADA) at the intersection of Lemerand Drive and Archer Road. The RTS Shuttle service costs $10 a game. Service is offered from three hours before the game until kickoff, with return shuttles beginning in the fourth quarter. For more information, call 352-334-2600 or go to www.go-rts.com.

TRADITIONS

The Boys from Old Florida: At the end of the third quarter, the University of Florida Fightin' Gator Marching Band plays, "We Are the Boys from Old Florida." Gator fans stand and sway left and right, arms locked, while singing the song.

Gatorade: The famous sports drink was invented by a team of researchers at the University of Florida in 1965 after a request for a hydrating drink by a Florida assistant coach who believed players needed something besides water to replace body fluids during practice and games in the hot weather. Gatorade was given credit by the football team for the Gators' 27-12 victory over Georgia Tech in the 1967 Orange Bowl during a 9-2 season. The drink caught on initially with University of Richmond and Miami (Ohio) and then spread to other schools and even to the professional football ranks.

B-BALL, ETC.

Coach Billy Donovan came to town in 1996 and made the Gators a national basketball power in only a few short years. By 2000, Donovan had Florida in the NCAA title game where the Gators lost to Michigan State. Florida claimed back-to-back NCAA basketball titles in 2006 and 2007. In doing so, Donovan's Gators became only the second school since UCLA from 1964 to 1975 (ten titles in twelve years) to win back-to-back national titles (Duke did it in 1991 and 1992). In March 2012, Florida made it all the way to the Elite Eight before falling to Louisville. Overall, Florida's athletic department is one of the best in America. Through 2010-11, Florida is the only school in the country to rank in the top ten in the annual All-Sports competition every year since 1983-84.

ABOUT TOWN

Gainesville is a youthful city, as evidenced by its median age of twenty-five. The sprawling University of Florida is a major employer in the area along with Shands Hospital. The city fathers and developers over the years have preserved many of the historic buildings in the city. A plethora of parks and lakes have provided entertainment possibilities and allowed the natural beauty of the area to remain in effect. Though land-locked, Gainesville still benefits from Gulf breezes. Summer days are warm, but the nights are cool. The winters are mild.

LODGING

Football weekends usually fill up early. Contact 866-778-5002 for room availability or go to www.visitgainesville.com/stay/special-event-accommodations.

Magnolia Plantation Bed & Breakfast Inn and Cottages: This Victorian Painted Lady, built in 1885, is less than two miles from campus. It features beautiful gardens, a central foyer, period kitchen, formal dining room, two sitting rooms, and five guest rooms. The separate cottages may require a two-night minimum stay. Run by Florida graduates. Full breakfast each morning. Snacks and beverages available during the day. There's a social hour nightly. *309 SE 7th St., Gainesville, FL 32601, 352-375-6653, www.magnoliabnb.com*

Best Western Plus Gateway Grand: A ways from campus, but a nice hotel for a weekend. Suites available. Sports bar and a spa on site as well. Access to nearby health club. Complimentary breakfast and free airport transportation. *4200 NW 97th Blvd., Gainesville, FL 32606, 352-331-3336, www. gatewaygrand.com*

Reitz Union Hotel: Located conveniently on the University of Florida campus, this thirty-six-room hotel is sold out months in advance on football weekends: minimum two-night stay (Friday and Saturday); reservation priority for football weekends is determined by a lottery. Lottery applications may be requested by telephone, email, or U.S. mail. Lottery applications are available early January each year. Lottery applications must be postmarked or e-mailed by April 1. Notification of lottery results will be sent out by May 1. Total advance payment for all reserved rooms will be due by June 1 to hold rooms. *Museum Rd. at Reitz Union Dr., Gainesville, FL 32611, 352-392-2151, www.union.ufl.edu/UnionHotel*

EATING

Joe's Place: Casual dining with wide range of appetizers, specialty salads, and sandwiches. Large pasta menu. Burgers are a specialty. Vegetarian dishes available. Signature steaks. A few fish and chicken entrees. Early Bird specials. *5109 NW 39th Ave., Gainesville, FL 32606, 352-377-7665, www. panamajoesplace.com*

101 Downtown: A lively bar, with drink specials pretty much daily. But the menu is solid with fish-dominated appetizers, and sushi and flatbreads for starters. Then finish off with a nice pasta, a steak, or a seafood dish or grab a burger. No entrée hits $30 on the menu. Establishment offers brunch from 11 a.m. until 4 p.m. every Sunday, with reservations recommended. *201 SE 2nd Ave., Gainesville, FL 32601, 352-376-4177, www.101gainesville.com*

Gator's Dockside: Wings, ribs, seafood, and sports is how this Florida chain describes itself. Gator's Dockside has big screen TVs to cater to the sports fan before and after the game they attend. Happy Hour specials Monday-Friday. Pool tables and video games. The signature grilled wings are flavored with fifteen different sauces in this bar restaurant which had its beginnings in Jacksonville in 1991. *3842 Newberry Rd., Ste 1 A, Gainesville, FL 32607, 352-338-4445, www.gatorsdockside.com*

SIGHTSEEING

Dudley Farm Historic State Park: Located in Newberry and open 9 a.m. - 4 p.m. Wed.-Sun., this is an 1880s working farmstead with visitor center, picnic area, trail, and self-guided tour of the original farmstead. Fee of $5 per car (up to eight occupants). *Located on State Route 26 Newberry Rd., four miles east of Newberry and seven miles west of I-75 (exit 387), 352-472-1142, www.friendsofdudleyfarm.org*

Paynes Prairie: This 30,000-acre wetlands preserve on the outskirts of Gainesville features a wide variety of wildlife, including bison, wild horses, alligators, sand hill cranes, eagles, herons, and much more. There are several lookout points and towers for viewing wildlife. Open during daylight hours year-around. Various token fees apply. *100 Savannah Blvd., Micanopy, FL 32667, 352-466-3397, www.floridastateparks.org/paynesprairie*

The Devil's Millhopper: This is a sinkhole that has now become a Natural Preserve and State Historic Site and Park. The highlight is a wooden-plank walkway that goes 120 feet down into the bottom of the sinkhole. "Small streams trickle down the steep slopes of the limestone sinkhole, disappearing through crevices in the ground. Lush vegetation thrives in the shade of the walls even in dry summers," according to the park's website. Picnicking spots available nearby. Open 9 a.m. - 5 p.m. Wed.-Sun., $4 per vehicle (up to eight people); $2 for pedestrians, cyclists. *4732 Millhopper Rd., Gainesville, FL 32653, 352-955-2008, www.floridastateparks.org/devilsmillhopper*

SHOPPING

The Gator Shop: Since 1946, this staple at the University of Florida has been selling fans Gator gear. Just about anything you can think of from bedroom accessories to memorabilia, some items signed by Gator coaching and playing greats! *1702 West University Ave., Ste. A-1, Gainesville, FL 32603, 352-376-5191*

Thornebrook Gallery and other stores in Thornebrook Village: Connecting breezeways and alcoves adorn this open-air village. Art galleries, rare gems, antiques and collectibles, specialty furniture, custom framing, designer eyewear, fine dining, and boutiques. *Gallery: 2441-6D NW 43rd St., Gainesville, FL 32606, 352-378-4947, www.thornebrookgallery.com*

NIGHTLIFE

Back Stage Lounge: Rock, metal, punk, garage bands are the staples for a bar that is open every night of the week, closing at 11 p.m. on Sundays, but open until 2 a.m. the other six days. Drink specials and happy hours. Pool, darts, and video games also are entertaining sidelights for a bar that is not for the conservative music fan. *1315 S. Main St., Gainesville, FL 32601, 352-378-9185, www.backstagelounge.info*

XS: Dancing with the college scene, but maybe worth a look. Frenzied crowd with the 1980s music blaring on into the night. Open three nights. Doesn't open until 10 p.m. and you can dance until 2 a.m. on Wednesday, Friday, and Saturday nights. *1728 W. University Ave., Gainesville, FL 32603, 352-377-7333*

TRAVELING TO GAINESVILLE?

Better book a flight because this is the farthest trip for Missouri fans in the SEC, roughly one thousand miles from Columbia to Florida's campus. The nearest major airport is Jacksonville International, about eighty miles northeast of Gainesville. Gainesville Regional Airport is another option, but fliers must make a connection through Atlanta, Charlotte, or Miami. The Mizzou Alumni Association hosts a Tiger Tailgate. Visit MizzouSportsTravel.com for more information on tickets and pricing.

GEORGIA

What sets the University of Georgia apart from many SEC schools is that the town of Athens was founded as the site for the university. The 1785 Georgia General Assembly charter to create the university stayed on paper for sixteen years until a five-man delegation selected a site in the summer of 1801. One of the men in the group, John Milledge, purchased 633 acres of land, named it Athens for the Greek city that was a renowned center of culture, and donated it for the university site. Four years later, the University of Georgia had its first graduating class, and two years after that Athens became officially incorporated.

Though no battles took place in Athens during the Civil War and because the university closed for three years in 1863 to house Confederate soldiers and refugees, it wasn't damaged like many other Southern schools. Boosted by federal dollars because it

UNIVERSITY OF GEORGIA

Students: 25,947

Athens: pop. 115,452

Sanford Stadium: seats 92,746

Colors: Red and Black

Nickname: Bulldogs

Mascot: Uga

Campus Attractions: The University of Georgia Museum of Art, Butts-Mehre Heritage Hall Sports Museum

Phone: 706-348-6010 (general information)
706-542-2200 (campus police for emergencies)
706-542-5813 (campus police for records and non-emergencies)
706-542-9036 (athletic department)

Tickets: 706-542-1231 or 877-542-1231 georgiadogs.com/tickets/geo-tickets. html

was declared a land-grant institution, the university re-opened in 1866. Along with the town, it flourished.

Chemistry professor Charles Herty brought football to the university in 1891. Guided by Walter Camp's instructional football book, Herty lined off a field on Georgia's quadrangle among three buildings and began teaching the sport. The Bulldogs' first game in 1892 was a 50-0 home victory over Mercer. Georgia joined the Southern Intercollegiate Athletic Association when it formed in 1894, but the football program was almost eliminated in 1897 when the Georgia State Legislature passed a bill making it illegal for state schools to play football. The legislation was a reaction to the death of Richard Gammon, a Georgia player who passed away on October 30 of that year from injuries sustained in a game against Virginia. But after Gammon's mother Rosalind wrote a letter to Georgia governor W. Y. Atkinson, pleading that he not sign the bill because her son truly had loved playing football, the governor never raised his pen and the bill died.

As the years passed, Georgia made some interesting head coaching hires, but clearly the two best were Wally Butts and Vince Dooley, hired in 1939 and 1964 respectively without any previous head coaching experience whatsoever.

Butts brought the passing game to Southern football and recruited multi-talented offensive threats like 1942 Heisman winner Frank Sinkwich and 1946 Maxwell winner Charlie Trippi.

By the time Butts finished his twenty-two-year coaching career, he had won four SEC titles and a national championship in 1942. He had left a legacy that seemed impossible to top until Georgia did something that would never be done in today's game. It hired a thirty-one-year-old whose coaching experience began and ended as Auburn's freshman coach. But twenty-five seasons later, that hiring of Dooley, who won six SEC championships and a

PROGRAM HIGHLIGHTS

NATIONAL CHAMPIONSHIPS (2): 1942, 1980

SEC CHAMPIONSHIPS (12): 1942, 1946 (tie), 1948, 1959, 1966 (tie), 1968, 1976 (tie), 1980, 1981 (tie), 1982, 2002, 2005

BOWL RECORD: 26-18-3 (.563). Last bowl—Lost 33-30 in three overtimes to Michigan State in 2012 Outback Bowl

LONGEST WINNING STREAK: 17 games (twice), 1945-47

WINNINGEST COACH: Vince Dooley (1964-88), 201-77-10, 71.5 percent

HEISMAN TROPHY WINNERS OR HIGHEST HEISMAN FINISH: Halfback Frank Sinkwich, 1942 winner; running back Herschel Walker, 1982 winner

national title in 1980, as well as becoming the ninth coach in Division I history to win more than two hundred games, was sheer genius.

Since Dooley's resignation in 1993—after his eleventh season with nine or more wins—the Bulldogs have had three coaches, including current boss Mark Richt. Richt, starting his twelfth season in 2012 as the dean of the SEC coaches, won league championships in 2002 and 2005, and his 11-2 2007 team finished with a No. 2 ranking.

LEGENDS

Vince Dooley

A fierce competitor and extraordinary gentleman, Dooley is the second winningest SEC coach in history with 201 victories in twenty-five seasons. Along the way, he coached forty All-Americans including 1982 Heisman Trophy winner . . .

Herschel Walker

The biggest, baddest man ever to play running back in the SEC, Walker was a chiseled 6-2, 222-pound physical specimen who still holds ten league records, such as career records for rushing yards (5,259 in just three seasons), yards per game (159.4), and rushing attempts per game (30.1).

Frank Sinkwich

Sinkwich capped a glorious career by winning the 1942 Heisman Trophy as captain of an 11-1 Georgia team that beat UCLA in the Rose Bowl.

Larry Munson

Georgia's gravelly throated, unabashed "homer" football radio play-by-play announcer was on-air for forty-two years until his death in November 2011. Few guys calling games ever showed more dramatic emotion swings than Munson.

STADIUM

Sanford Stadium: Sunken solidly in firm Georgia red clay, 92,746-seat Sanford Stadium is named for the late Dr. S. V. Sanford, former school president and chancellor of the university system. Inside the stadium near Gate 1, a mausoleum contains the remains of all Georgia's English Bulldog mascots (known as Ugas) that have gone to that great kennel in the sky.

FIGHT SONG

"GLORY"

(Played after a score and sung to the tune of the "Battle Hymn of the Republic")

Glory, glory to old Georgia!

Glory, glory to old Georgia!

Glory, glory to old Georgia!

G-E-O-R-G-I-A.

Glory, glory to old Georgia!

Glory, glory to old Georgia!

Glory, glory to old Georgia!

G-E-O-R-G-I-A.

MASCOT

Georgia's line of live English Bulldog mascots known as Uga (pronounced UH-guh, though it's an abbreviation for University of Georgia) started in the mid-1950s. Savannah attorney and Georgia graduate Sonny Seiler (BBA '56, JD '57), has owned and raised all the Ugas since a family friend, Frank Heard, gave Seiler and his wife, Cecilia, a bulldog that soon became Uga I when the Seilers were still newlyweds in 1956. There's not another mascot that has attended a Heisman Trophy ceremony in New York City wearing a black bow tie and white collar (Uga IV) and who has his own room at the team's hotel for road games.

MIZZOU CONNECTION

All-time football record vs. Missouri: 1-0

1960: Georgia 14, Missouri 0 (Orange Bowl; Miami [1959 season])

Dan Devine's Tigers shut out four opponents during the 1959 regular season, but they were allergic to the end zone in Miami. In Missouri's first Orange Bowl appearance in twenty years, a couple Fran Tarkenton touchdown passes was all the fifth-ranked Bulldogs needed as MU finished the season 6-5. The Tigers were fortunate to be in Miami in the first place: Big Eight champion Oklahoma qualified for the Orange Bowl but had played there the year before, and conference rules prohibited a team from making back-to-back appearances in the same bowl. The Tigers actually outgained Wallace Butts' SEC champion Bulldogs in total yardage, 260-216.

Marked man: When Missouri needed a football coach after the 2000 season, a star-in-waiting emerged at Florida State, Seminoles offensive coordinator and quarterback specialist Mark Richt. MU contacted four candidates, including Richt, who interviewed with school officials at an off-site location. "My wife and I thought a lot about going to Columbia," Richt said in November 2011. "We had a lot of positive thoughts and feelings about going to Missouri." Instead, Richt accepted Georgia's offer and Missouri hired Toledo's Gary Pinkel. Twenty-five head coaches were hired that offseason, and only four are still on the job heading into the 2012 season, including Richt and Pinkel. The Tigers were scheduled to play their first SEC game against—you guessed it—Richt's Bulldogs on September 8 in Columbia. Once the season kicks off, Pinkel and Richt will be in their twelfth seasons at their respective schools, longer than any other coaches in the SEC.

Dawg catchers: In the span of four days in March 2001, Missouri's basketball teams vanquished higher-seeded teams from Georgia in both the men's and women's NCAA Tournaments. First, Quin Snyder's MU men toppled the Bulldogs in the first round in Greensboro, N.C. The bigger win came three days later, when MU's women stunned No. 2 seed Georgia—on the Bulldogs' home court in Athens—in a second-round upset that's widely considered the biggest win in team history. It propelled the Tigers into the Sweet Sixteen for the second time ever.

GAME DAY

MEDIA

Broadcasting the Game: WRFC-AM 960 in Athens is the hometown station, but WSB-AM 750 in Atlanta has a signal that can heard throughout the South at night.

Covering the Bulldogs: www.dogbytesonline.com (*Athens Banner-Herald*), www.ajc.com/sports/uga/ (*Atlanta Journal-Constitution*)

TAILGATING

Fans can't set up tailgates before 7 a.m. on game day and may not have any university electricity or cable hookups. Fans must provide their own power and video source. Tailgating in parking spaces is prohibited. On the part of Georgia's campus known as North Campus, tailgating is allowed to start five hours prior to kickoff. But North Campus tailgate rules are stingy, not allowing grills or cookers of any type, no household furniture (folding chairs are permissible), no TVs, no amplified music, no generators, no kegs.

SHUTTLE

Georgia's free Campus Transit provides game-day shuttles for fans parking in the East Campus Parking Deck/Ramsey Center area and Intramural Fields area that are located off College Station Road adjacent to Exit 7 from the 10 Loop. The shuttles, which drop fans at Gate 6 of Sanford Stadium, start five and a half hours before kickoff and run continuously until fifteen minutes before kickoff. Sanford Stadium doesn't open its gates until two hours before kickoff. After the game, return services to parking lots runs for two hours.

TRADITIONS

Between the hedges: Hedges have bordered the Sanford Stadium playing field since its opening day on October 29, 1929. When the 1996 Atlanta Summer Olympics scheduled their soccer medal games in Sanford Stadium, all the hedges had to be ripped out to fit in a regulation soccer field. The university avoided a PR problem with its tradition-loving fans when they discovered the hedges were diseased; therefore, the school had a reason to remove them. It's believed the term "between the hedges" was coined by famous sportswriter Grantland Rice when he worked for the *Atlanta Journal* early in his career. Former LSU coach Charles McClendon once said his team was "playing behind the bushes" when it traveled to Athens to battle the Bulldogs.

Ringing the chapel bell: Back in the 1890s, when the pre-Sanford Stadium football field was next to the campus chapel, Georgia upperclassmen ordered freshmen to sprint to the chapel immediately after every Bulldogs victory and ring the chapel bell until midnight. Now after a Georgia victory, any fan or student can stop in at the chapel, give a couple of tugs, and ring the bell.

B-BALL, ETC.

Georgia has had some terrific athletes pass through its doors, such as nine-time NBA All-Star Dominique Wilkins, nine-time Pro Bowl quarterback Fran Tarkenton, four-time Olympic Gold Medalist women's basketball star Teresa Edwards and pro golfer Bubba Watson, who won the green jacket at the 2012 Masters. But no college women's gymnastic program has won more national championships than the ten captured by Georgia's Gym Dogs, including five straight national titles from 2005 to 2009.

ALL HAIL TO DEAR OLD UGA!

ABOUT TOWN

Each SEC town has its own personality, but none is as artsy and diverse as Athens, part Antebellum and part funk. The "Old South" architecture has always been there, but starting in the late 1970s, thanks to Athens-based bands R.E.M. and the B-52s, the town blew up into a mecca for aspiring musicians. *Rolling Stone Magazine* even named Athens as the No. 1 College Music Scene in America. The creative juices spread, attracting culinary whizzes, clothing designers, almost anybody thinking outside of the box. There is a vibe that seems to get stronger every year.

LODGING

Foundry Park Inn and Spa: A boutique inn with about 120 rooms, Foundry Park's Southern Colonial architecture with detailed touches such as plantation-style shutters are the first hints that this is no ordinary hotel. *295 E. Dougherty St., Athens, GA 30601, 706-549-7020, www.foundryparkinn.com*

Magnolia Terrace Guest House: A Colonial Revival bed and breakfast with eight guest rooms, Magnolia Terrace has the best linens, softest down pillows and comforters, private clawfoot tubs, and antiques galore. *277 Hill St., Athens, GA 30601, 706-548-3860*

The Georgia Conference Center and Hotel: A 200-room on-campus hotel, just a short walk from Sanford Stadium, the Georgia Conference Center and Hotel has everything needed for a great stay, including a collection of four unique dining options. *1197 South Lumpkin St., Athens, GA 30602, 706-548-1311, www. georgiacenter.uga.edu/cch/dining*

EATING

DePalma's Italian Café: Three locations, but the one downtown is a must for football fans. Extremely reasonable prices and a different type lasagna is made fresh daily. *401 E. Broad St., Athens, GA 30601, 706-354-6966, www. depalmasitaliancafe.com*

Last Resort Grill: Originally a music club that opened in 1966, it was closed for a decade before being re-born into a grill serving some of the most creative dishes in Athens, like the bacon-filled gourmet meatloaf topped with Serrano-mint jam. *174-184 W. Clayton St., Athens, GA 30601, 706-549-0810, www.lastresortgrill.com*

The Varsity: You go to Athens and you've got to stop in at The Varsity, which has been cranking out chili dogs for the students and townspeople since 1932. Throw caution and your diet to the wind, and eat for the cycle by adding an order of onion rings and a frosted orange drink. Your eyes will roll to the back of your head. *1000 West Broad St., Athens, GA 30606, 706-548-6325 or 800-273-4690, www.thevarsity.com*

SIGHTSEEING

Historic Athens tour: Conducted by Classic City Tours, this ninety-minute bus tour runs daily (except for Tuesday and Thursday) from the Athens Welcome Center starting at 2 p.m. Tour sites include historic neighborhoods, downtown Athens, and highlighted points of interest around the University of Georgia. Cost is $15 per person. *Classic City Tours, 280 E. Dougherty St. at Athens Welcome Center, Athens, GA 30601, 706-208-8687, www.athenswelcomecenter.com*

World of Wonder Community Playground: If you've made a long drive to Athens stuck in a vehicle with a bunch of kids, what better place to turn them loose than Georgia's largest community-built playground, free to the public. Its two acres are packed with swings, climbing walls, tunnels, bridges, slides, mazes, and playscapes. *4440 Lexington Rd., Southeast Clarke Park, Athens, GA 30601, 706-613-3871, www.visitathensga.com*

SHOPPING

Helix: A 5,000-square-foot store full of practical and quirky items to fit every lifestyle and drug hallucination. Are you dying to bring home a samurai umbrella or a redneck wine glass (a mason jar sitting atop a glass stem)? *146 E. Clayton St., Athens, GA 30601, 706-354-8631, www.helixathens.com*

Pints and Paints: It's an art studio . . . and it also has a license to sell beer and wine. You don't even need artistic ability, because an instructor will guide you through a painting that fits your skill level. And if you drink enough, whatever you paint, you'll think you're Billy Bob Picasso. *The Leathers Building, Suite 600, 675 Pulaski St., Athens, GA 30601, 706-850-7200, www.pintsandpaints.com*

Georgia Square Mall: Just to cover all your shopping bases, there are more than sixty stores. *3700 Atlanta Highway, Athens, GA 30606, 706-543-7908, www.georgiasquaremall.com*

NIGHTLIFE

40 Watt Club: Named by Gibson Guitars as one of the top ten greatest rock venues of all-time, acts like R.E.M., the Indigo Girls, and the B-52's began in this club that still rocks. *285 W. Washington St., Athens, GA 30601, 706-549-7871, www.40watt.com*

Blind Pig Tavern: A helluva good sports bar. If you get the Ninja chicken wings (the hottest available) and they begin to melt your lips, you can't send 'em back for a refund. The fine print on the menu reads, "NO REFUND ON WINGS IF THEY ARE TOO HOT FOR YOUR TASTE." So suck it up and order colder beer. *Two locations but one closest to the Georgia campus is 485 Baldwin St., Athens, GA 30605, 706-548-3442, www.blindpigtavern.com*

The Georgia Theatre: Hundreds and hundreds of bands have played in this revamped 1930s-40s-style theatre. Some you've heard of (B.B. King, Lady Antebellum) and many you haven't (ZZ Topless, Future Ape Tapes). *215 N. Lumpkin St., Athens, GA 30601, 706-850-7670, www.georgiatheatre.com*

TRAVELING TO ATHENS?

From Missouri, your best bet is to fly into Hartsfield-Jackson Atlanta International Airport and make the eighty-mile drive into Athens. St. Louis, Kansas City, and Columbia offer direct flights into Atlanta, while Columbia also offers regular service through Memphis International, where you can pick up an Atlanta connection. If you don't mind a connection or two, Augusta Regional Airport, about one hundred miles away from UGA, is another option. By car, Athens is a haul from Missouri, at least a thirteen-hour drive from Columbia. The Mizzou Alumni Association hosts a Tiger Tailgate. Visit MizzouSportsTravel.com for more information on tickets and pricing.

KENTUCKY

The University of Kentucky, founded in 1865 as a land-grant institution near downtown Lexington, started with 190 students and 10 professors. Kentucky University had been established in Harrodsburg in 1858 and seven years later merged with Transylvania University to form the current school.

Kentucky was the first Southeastern Conference team to introduce football (in 1881). And eleven years later, Kentucky adopted blue and white for its colors, dropping yellow for white.

"The Immortals," the 1898 University of Kentucky football squad (7-0-0), still remains as the only undefeated, untied, and unscored-upon Wildcats football team. The Immortals outscored opponents, 180-0. The closest game was a 6-0 victory over Centre College.

Kentucky played its first homecoming game on November 25, 1915, and defeated Tennessee, 6-0. The first night home game in University of Kentucky history occurred on October 5, 1929, at old Stoll Field when the Wildcats topped Maryville, 40-0.

UNIVERSITY OF KENTUCKY

Students: 27,000

Lexington: pop. 295,803

Commonwealth Stadium: seats 67,942

Colors: Blue and White

Nickname: Wildcats

Mascot: Blue, Wildcat, Scratch

Campus Attractions: The Art Museum at the University of Kentucky; K-Lair Grill (Campus Greasy Spoon since the 1960s)

Phone: 859-257-9000 (general information)
859-257-8573 (campus police)
859-257-8000 (athletic department)

Tickets: May be purchased online through Ticketmaster.com, over the phone by calling 800-928-2287, or in person at the Joe Craft Center ticket office.

Perhaps the greatest Kentucky team of the modern era was in 1950 when the Wildcats won one of their two SEC football titles. Coached by Paul "Bear" Bryant, who later would lead Alabama to great heights, the Wildcats finished the regular season with a 10-1 record and then ended Oklahoma's thirty-one-game winning streak with a 13-7 victory over the Sooners in the 1951 Sugar Bowl. The following season Bryant took the Wildcats to the Cotton Bowl in Dallas, where they defeated TCU, 20-7, behind quarterback Babe Parilli.

Bryant left Kentucky for Texas A&M after eight consecutive winning seasons and four bowl trips. Kentucky had much more modest success under its next three coaches. During that era, the Wildcats' Nat Northington was the first African-American player to sign with a Southeastern Conference school and the first to play in a league contest—against Ole Miss in 1967.

Fran Curci spent nine seasons in Lexington (1973-81), won Kentucky's second SEC title, but also put the Wildcats on an NCAA probation that cost them a bowl berth in 1977. Still, such players as Sonny Collins, Warren Bryant, Art Still, and Derrick Ramsey were stars during Curci's tenure.

In 1976, the Curci-led Wildcats tied Georgia for the SEC title, posted a 9-3 record, and defeated North Carolina, 21-0, in the Peach Bowl. The following season, Kentucky was unbeaten in SEC play but ineligible to go to a bowl or win the SEC because of the NCAA probation.

Before the 1982 season, former Wildcat player Jerry Clairborne returned to coach his alma mater. He took the Wildcats to a couple of bowls during his eight seasons, in 1983 and 1984, after inheriting Curci's probation, but could post only one more winning record through the 1989 season before he left. Coach Bill Curry had just one bowl trip and one winning season from 1990 to 1996.

In 1997, Kentucky's football program got an offensive shot to its system when Hal Mumme brought his wide-open passing attack to town. It worked for a

PROGRAM HIGHLIGHTS

NATIONAL CHAMPIONSHIPS (1): 1950

SEC CHAMPIONSHIPS (2): 1950, 1976

BOWL RECORD: 8-7 (.533). Last bowl—A 27-10 loss to Pittsburgh in the 2010 BBVA Compass Bowl

LONGEST WINNING STREAK: 12 games (1909-10)

WINNINGEST COACH (BEST PERCENTAGE WITH MORE THAN THREE YEARS AT SCHOOL): Paul "Bear" Bryant (1946-53), 60-23-5, 71.0 percent

HEISMAN TROPHY WINNERS OR HIGHEST HEISMAN FINISH: Quarterback Babe Parilli, third in 1951

couple of bowl trips. And in 1998, quarterback Tim Couch was a fourth-place finisher for the Heisman and SEC Player of the Year. And Kentucky played in its first New Year's Day game in forty-seven years, the Outback Bowl.

After the brief Guy Morriss era ended in NCAA probation, Rich Brooks took over in 2003 as coach. After three straight losing seasons, he became the first Kentucky coach to go to four straight bowls as well as the first coach to win three straight before retiring and being replaced by his assistant Joker Phillips. Phillips' teams have finished fifth in the SEC East each of his first two seasons.

LEGENDS

Bob Gain

The school's only Outland Trophy winner (best interior lineman) in 1950, Gain was also the first player from the Southeastern Conference to win the award, which originated in 1946. He was a two-time All-American.

Babe Parilli

Parilli was a two-time All-American from the same era as Gain. He completed 331 of 592 passes for 4,351 yards and 50 touchdowns during his career. He took the Wildcats to three straight bowls.

Howard Schnellenberger

Schnellenberger later would win a national championship as coach of the Miami Hurricanes In 1983, but he was a standout end for the Wildcats in the mid-1950s and was named an All-American in 1955. He had one touchdown catch for every four receptions as a Wildcat.

George Blanda

At Kentucky, Blanda lettered as a quarterback, punter, and kicker for four seasons (1945-48). The Pro Football Hall of Famer became the first player in pro football to score two thousand points in a career.

NOTABLE ALUMS

Ashley Judd—Actress who frequents Wildcat basketball games

Happy Chandler—Former commissioner of Major League Baseball who integrated the sport

Brady Deaton—University of Missouri chancellor who orchestrated the school's move to the SEC

James Host—Founder of Host Communications

STADIUM

Commonwealth: The stadium opened in 1973 after the Wildcats left their previous home of forty-eight years at Stoll Field/McLean Stadium. The team has only had one unbeaten season at Commonwealth (5-0) in 1977. The stadium is situated on what was once the University of Kentucky Experimental Station Farm Grounds. A major renovation occurred in 1999 when both ends of the stadium were enclosed, and about ten thousand seats and forty suites added.

MASCOT

The University of Kentucky actually has three mascots: the Wildcat, Scratch, and Blue. Since a road football victory at Illinois in 1909, the school has been associated with the Wildcats nickname.

The Wildcat human mascot dates to 1976-77 when Gary Tanner donned the costume and headdress and entertained at athletic events. Scratch, another costumed mascot, was unveiled two decades later and interacts more with children.

Blue is the current bobcat mascot and lives in the Kentucky Department of Fish and Wildlife's Salato Wildlife Center three miles west of Frankfort on U.S. Route 60. It never attends games because of its shy nature and dislike for crowds. The public can actually see Blue at the center. Over the years Kentucky has had several other animal mascots. Tom was given to the university in 1921. Other live mascots followed, including TNT, Whiskers, Hot Tamale, and Colonel.

MIZZOU CONNECTION

All-time football record vs. Missouri: 2-1

1904: Missouri 37, Kentucky 6 (Columbia)

1965: Kentucky 7, Missouri 0 (Columbia)

1968: Kentucky 12, Missouri 6 (Lexington)

Like it's been for most of its existence, Kentucky was a middling SEC program in the 1960s when the Wildcats inexplicably swept Dan Devine's powerhouse from the Big Eight. In the first meeting, the first in a newly

Courtesy Mizzou Athletics Media Relations

expanded Memorial Stadium, the Tigers' offense struggled in the sweltering Columbia heat. Kentucky wasn't much better, as the *Columbia Daily Tribune* reported UK coach Charlie Bradshaw "hadn't much to say about the Wildcats' offense, except that it was terrible." Three years later Missouri opened the season in Lexington and debuted its new I-formation offense, along with junior college transfers Mel Gray, a blazing receiver, and quarterback Terry McMillan. Still, MU couldn't overcome four turnovers and three missed field goals.

Ford pick-up: Travis Ford was named to the All-Big Eight Freshman Team for the 1989-90 season after setting Missouri freshman records for assists and steals while splitting time in a potent backcourt with Lee Coward and Anthony Peeler. He was so popular, a campus publication ran a poll asking students to choose a nickname for the brilliant shooter. The choices: Hot Rod, Turbo, Maverick, Scooter, Sparky, Ford Dog, and Napoleon. Ford soon became known as Traitor Travis. After his rookie campaign, the Madisonville, Kentucky, native returned home to play for Rick Pitino at Kentucky, citing turmoil between MU's faculty and coaches and possible NCAA sanctions. At Kentucky, Ford became a star and twice earned All-SEC honors.

Deaton delivers: If there's one person responsible for Missouri joining the SEC, it was university chancellor Brady Deaton, whose alma mater is . . . Kentucky. Raised on a farm in Pine Grove, Kentucky, Deaton once described himself to the *Columbia Daily Tribune* as a "hillbilly from the Appalachian region." He'd go on to earn a degree in agricultural economics at UK and later a master of arts in diplomacy and international commerce. Deaton found himself in a delicate position during conference realignment, serving as both MU's chancellor and chairman of the Big 12 board of directors. Deaton eventually negotiated MU's way into the SEC, leaning on his close association with several powerbrokers across the league, including Florida president Bernie Machen.

GAME DAY

MEDIA

Broadcasting the Game: WLAP-AM 630 and WBUL-FM 98.1 in Lexington, along with WHAS-AM 840 in Louisville

Covering the Wildcats: www.kentucky.com (*Lexington Herald-Leader*), www.courier-journal.com/section/SPORTS (*Louisville Courier-Journal*)

TAILGATING

Cooper Drive Tailgate & Parking: Tailgate setups and parking vehicles may begin no earlier than noon on Fridays prior to game day. Beginning at noon on Friday, two vehicles will be permitted to parallel park outside, along the painted six-foot restraining line within each designated tailgate box/area. Vehicles will be restricted from parking in any water retention ditches, flood areas, sidewalks, and otherwise marked-off areas.

SHUTTLE

Game-day shuttles operate between campus and downtown Lexington and Commonwealth Stadium. Cost for both the UK Football Express—Campus Route and the UK Football Express—Downtown Route is $1 one-way and $2 round trip. Stops are at Cooper Drive/ University Drive; in front of the Kentucky Clinic; and at Rose Street/Huguelet Drive.

TRADITIONS

"My Old Kentucky Home" is played at each Wildcat football game, and Kentucky fans sing along with the song written by Stephen Foster in 1853 and adopted as the state song in 1928. It is also sung each year at the Kentucky Derby:

> *The sun shines bright on my old Kentucky home,*
> *'Tis summer, the people are gay;*
> *The corntop's ripe and the meadows in the bloom,*
> *While the birds make music all the day.*
> *The young folks roll on the little cabin floor,*
> *All merry, all happy, and bright;*
> *By-n-by hard times come a-knocking at the door,*
> *Then, my old Kentucky home, good-night!*
> *Weep no more, my lady,*
> *Oh! Weep no more, today!*
> *We will sing one song for my old Kentucky home,*
> *For my old Kentucky home far away.*

Governor's Cup: The Governor's Cup goes each year to the winner of the Kentucky-Louisville football game, which is usually played in late August or early September. The series, after a seventy-year layoff, was resumed in 1994. Since then, Louisville holds a 10-8 advantage in the eighteen games played. The Cardinals won 24-17 in Lexington in 2011 to snap Kentucky's four-game winning streak in the series.

B-BALL, ETC.

To say basketball is king in the Bluegrass State is an understatement. Once upon a time, Kentucky was about the only school that took the sport seriously in the Southeastern Conference. That has changed over the years, of course, with Florida and Arkansas winning national championships in the last two decades. But Kentucky's men's basketball program annually is one of the tops in the country and claimed the 2012 NCAA title. The Wildcats have won eight NCAA titles since the tournament began in 1939, trailing only UCLA (11) in championships won.

Kentucky also has one of the best cheerleading squads in college sports. Last January, for a record nineteenth time, the Wildcats won the national cheerleading title at the ESPN Wide World of Sports in Orlando, Florida. Kentucky finished ahead of second-place Alabama, who ended a streak of three consecutive Kentucky titles in 2011. Kentucky has failed to win the title just three times since 1995.

ABOUT TOWN

Lexington is located the middle of horse country. If you arrive by plane at the Lexington Airport, a cluster of horse farms greet you. This bluegrass region is noted for its rolling plateau, beauty, fertile soil, and excellent pastureland.

Bourbon distillerys are plentiful as well. Founded in 1775, seventeen years before Kentucky became a state, Lexngton is also noted for tobacco farms and hand-crafts. In recent years, Kentucky's second-largest city has become more diversi-fied in employment: General Electric, UPS, and Long John Silver's are some of the largest employers. The University of Kentucky, although the largest and most prestigious school in the area, is just one of about fifteen colleges or universities.

LODGING

Football weekends usually fill up early. For room availability, go to www.commercelexington.com/HotelsMotels.

University Inn: Centrally located between the airport and the major UK sports facilities, including Commonwealth Stadium, which is within walking distance, this three-story, ninety-room hotel offers complimentary continental breakfast. The hotel was built in 1998. *1229 S. Limestone St., Lexington, KY 40503, 859-278-6625, www.uinn.biz*

Marriott Griffin Gate Resort: A little on the pricey side, but you would enjoy a picturesque part of Lexington with a football or basketball weekend stay here. Indulge. There's an 18-hole golf course and a luxurious full-service spa on the premises. And the service of the 400-plus room hotel is five-star. *1800 Newtown Pike, Lexington, KY 40511, 859-231-5100, www.marriott.com/hotels/travel/lexky-griffin-gate-marriott-resort-and-spa/*

Hilton Lexington/Downtown: The hotel is central to attractions, restaurants, shopping, museums, and entertainment venues, including Ashland, the Henry Clay Estate, Keeneland Race Course, Kentucky Horse Park, University of Kentucky, Shaker Village, and the Historic Bourbon Trail, according to the hotel website. A full-service hotel with all the trimmings. *369 West Vine Street, Lexington, KY 40507, 859-231-9000, www.lexingtondowntownhotel.com*

EATING

Natasha's Bistro & Bar: By its own advertisement "Kentucky's premiere arts and entertainment restaurant, serving New American Cuisine, and known for contemporary dining with a lively venue of theater and music." Lots of dishes with Greek and Middle Eastern influence. *112 Esplanade at Main St., Lexington, KY 40507, 859-259-2754, www.beetnik.com*

The Ketch Seafood Grill: It has the smell of a fish house, so it must be good. Dated décor makes a patron feel like he's back in the 1970s. This has been a staple of the Lexington scene for awhile for those who like fresh seafood. Wood-grilled seafood, steaks, ribs, and chicken. *2012 Regency Rd., Lexington, KY 40503, 859-277-5919, www.ketchseafoodgrill.com*

Billy's Bar-B-Q: Voted the best barbeque in Lexington by one publication. The place has been open since 1978 and serves real pit barbeque—ribs, pulled pork, beef brisket, mutton, and chicken wings. Kentucky Burgoo, a traditional meat and vegetable stew, is a specialty. *101 Cochran Rd., Lexington, KY 40502, 859-269-9593, www.billysbarbq.com*

SIGHTSEEING

Shaker Village: A preserved site of the Shaker community takes you back in time to a simpler era. There's also an inn where visitors can stay and dine and appreciate this religious sect's history even more. *3501 Lexington Rd., Harrodsburg, KY 40330, 859-734-5411, www.shakervillageky.org*

Barrel House Distillery: Overview of the distilling process, a brief history of distilling in Lexington, and tastes of fine spirits. Hours: Noon to 5 p.m. Fridays, 11 a.m. to 3 p.m. Saturdays, or by appointment. *1200 Manchester St., Building #9, Lexington, KY 40504, 859-259-0159, www.barrelhousedistillery.com*

Kentucky Horse Park: Open seven days a week from March 15 to October 31, 9 to 5 daily. From November 1 to March 14 open Wednesday to Saturday. Same hours. Ticket prices vary seasonally. Various attractions including the International Museum of the Horse, Man o' War Memorial, the Farmer Shop, Big Barn, and more. *4089 Iron Works Parkway, Lexington, KY 40511, 859-233-4303, www.kyhorsepark.com*

SHOPPING

Victorian Square Shoppes: The Shoppes are connected to Triangle Center, the Hilton Lexington/Downtown, the Hyatt Regency, Lexington Convention Center, and the Shops at Lexington Center by covered walkway. Covered parking (three hours) is free with a validated ticket from any of the area's shops, restaurants, or bars, with no purchase necessary. *Intersection of Main St. and Broadway (U.S. Route 68) in the heart of downtown Lexington, 859-252-7575, www.victoriansquareshoppes.com*

Old Kentucky Candies: An array of goodies such as bourbon chocolates and cherries, mints, toffee, creams, and truffles. A place for those with a sweet tooth before or after the game. *450 Southland Dr., Lexington, KY 40503, 859-278-4444, www.oldkycandy.com*

UK Team Shop: If you want a souvenir from Wildcat country, this is the place to get it. Large selection of Big Blue items. *www.ukteamshop.com/wildcats/home.php*

NIGHTLIFE

Cheapside Bar & Grill: Voted the best bar and patio in Lexington by one publication. Patrons might be a little confused with all the themes: Southwestern dining room, Victorian pub, and Tropical patio. But there is a little something for everyone. Lots of drink specials. Live music at times. *Corner of Mill St. and Short, Lexington, KY 40507, 859-254-0046, www.promptsite.com/cheapside*

Forte: Dance club and live music venue in the heart of Chevy Chase area. It has the largest multi-level dance floor in Lexington, over 7,000 square feet. Doors don't open until 10 p.m. on Thursday and Friday, and 9 p.m. on Saturday. But you can boogie until 2:30 a.m. *815 E. Euclid Ave., Lexington, KY 40502, 859-335-0440, www.fortelex.com*

Redmon's: A local musician owns, operates, and entertains on stage in this club, which is below street level. The music is Southern rock and country. Lots of young professionals and college students who prefer to stand with their drinks, so you probably will, too, in the usually packed scene. Open Thursday-Saturday, 9 p.m. to 2:30 a.m. *269 W. Main St., Lexington, KY 40507, 859-252-5802, www.larryredmon.com*

TRAVELING TO LEXINGTON?

Lexington is a manageable drive from the Show-Me State, a straight shot across Highway 64 from St. Louis. UK is about 460 miles from Columbia and 340 from St. Louis. From Kansas City, you're looking at a ten-hour drive. Lexington Blue Grass Airport offers some direct flights but not to Missouri airports. Louisville International Airport is sixty miles to the west of Lexington and offers direct flights to St. Louis and connecting flights to Kansas City and Springfield. The Mizzou Alumni Association hosts a Tiger Tailgate. Visit MizzouSportsTravel.com for more information on tickets and pricing.

LSU

LSU opened its doors in Pineville, Louisiana, in 1860 as the Louisiana State Seminary of Learning and Military Academy. The school closed for two years from 1863 to 1865 but was burned down in 1869. At that point, the university was moved to Baton Rouge and its name changed to Louisiana State University. In 1926, after four years of construction, LSU opened its current campus. The school seemed to be floundering, with not even two thousand students, when Louisiana governor Huey P. Long personally made the school the apple of his eye. He diverted $9 million of the state budget to buy more land for the school, build more buildings, add more teachers, and build a medical school.

Long was also smart enough to realize that athletics was a big part of a university attracting students. The school's football program had started back in 1893, brought to LSU by Dr. Charles Coates, a young chemistry professor from Baltimore who had played the

LOUISIANA STATE UNIVERSITY

Students: 28,985

Baton Rouge: pop. 229,553

Tiger Stadium: seats 92,542

Colors: Purple and Gold

Nickname: Tigers

Mascot: Mike the Tiger

Campus Attractions: Memorial, Mike the Tiger's habitat

Phone: 225-578-5030 (general information)
225-578-3231 (campus police)
225-578-8001 (athletic department)

Tickets: 225-578-2184 or
800-960-8587
www.lsutix.net

sport as a student at Johns Hopkins University. Yet LSU football didn't open eyes until the brash Long got involved in almost every phase. Before he was assassinated in 1935, Long was savvy enough to kill two birds with one stone. LSU's president said the school needed more dormitory rooms. Long wanted more seats in Tiger Stadium. When Long discovered the federal government would foot the bill for the construction of dormitory rooms through the Works Progress Administration, he found an architect to design a stadium expansion that added 24,000 seats, with 250 dorm rooms and 21 offices underneath the seats. The newly expanded Tiger Stadium opened in 1936, when LSU won the second of back-to-back SEC titles after joining the fledgling conference at its inception in 1933.

After 1936, LSU didn't win another SEC championship until 1958 when the Tigers won their first official national championship under fourth-year coach Paul Dietzel, hired in 1955 from Army where he was a line coach. Two years before Dietzel's hiring, LSU brought on Jim Corbett as athletic director.

Together, along with LSU sports information director Ace Higgins, they began building the program as a nationally recognized product. Corbett moved kickoff times to night, Dietzel was a superb recruiter and tactician, and Higgins was able to tap into the top national publications of the day, *Life Magazine* and *Look Magazine*. By 1959, LSU not only had a national title, but a Heisman Trophy winner in halfback Billy Cannon.

Since Dietzel left to become Army's coach in 1962, LSU has had eight head coaches, with two of them—Nick Saban and Les Miles—winning national championships in 2003 and 2007 respectively.

Through the years, all the LSU coaches have marveled at the passion of LSU fans, how there is no place better to play than in Tiger Stadium on a Saturday night.

That all started with the late Corbett, who once stated his purple-and-gold-

PROGRAM HIGHLIGHTS

NATIONAL CHAMPIONSHIPS (3): 1958, 2003, 2007

SEC CHAMPIONSHIPS (11): 1935, 1936, 1958, 1961 (tie), 1970, 1986, 1988 (tie), 2001, 2003, 2007, 2011

BOWL RECORD: 22-20-1 (.523). Last bowl—Lost 21-0 to Alabama in 2012 BCS national championship game

LONGEST WINNING STREAK: 19 games, 1958-59

WINNINGEST COACH: Charles McClendon (1962-79), 137-59-7, 69.2 percent

HEISMAN TROPHY WINNERS OR HIGHEST HEISMAN FINISH: Halfback Billy Cannon, 1959 winner

tinged vision in author Pete Finney's book *The Fighting Tigers*: "Because LSU grew up with Baton Rouge and Baton Rouge with LSU, there is a stronger personal identity than is found in most metropolitan areas. Local home boys from small communities stimulate civic pride and those communities carry that enthusiasm with them to Baton Rouge on Saturday night. What we have is the Great Society of Equality at work—the doctor, the lawyer, the farmer, the plant worker, the society matron—they all band together in a single social strata. In Baton Rouge, the average fan doesn't seem to have a good week in his job if the Tigers lose."

LEGENDS

Charles McClendon

A former player under Bear Bryant at Kentucky, the folksy McClendon is LSU's coaching leader in wins (137), bowl appearances (thirteen), and bowl victories (seven).

Billy Cannon

LSU's only Heisman Trophy winner was best known for his legendary game-winning eighty-nine-yard punt return against Ole Miss on Halloween night in 1959.

Jerry Stovall

A recruiting afterthought, Stovall was LSU's last signee in its fifty-two-member 1959 recruiting class. He developed into the most versatile player (halfback, safety, punter, and kickoff returner) in school history and finished second in the 1962 Heisman Trophy voting.

Tommy Casanova

As a three-time All-American defensive back from 1969 to 1971 who also was one of LSU's best punt returners in history, Casanova got more votes than any other player in Tigers history when LSU fans selected the school's modern-day All-Century team.

NOTABLE ALUMS

Bill Conti—Academy Award– and Emmy Award–winning composer

James Carville—Political commentator and consultant

Hubert Humphrey—Thirty-eighth vice president of the United States

Dr. James Andrews—Regarded as the nation's best orthopedic surgeon for sports-related injuries

---

STADIUM

Tiger Stadium: With 92,542-seat Tiger Stadium named in poll after poll as the scariest, loudest, most difficult college stadium in America, LSU's winning percentage through 2011 in this Cajun insane asylum nicknamed "Death Valley" is 72.2 percent. How loud can it get? When LSU scored the game-winning TD there against Auburn in 1988, the explosive crowd reaction caused an earth tremor that registered on a seismograph in LSU's Geology Department across campus.

FIGHT SONG

"VICTORY FOR LSU"

Like Knights of old, Let's fight to hold

The glory of the Purple Gold.

Let's carry through, Let's die or do

To win the game for dear old LSU.

Keep trying for that high score;

Come on and fight,

We want some more, some more.

Come on you Tigers, Fight! Fight! Fight!

for dear old L-S-U.

RAH!

MASCOTS

LSU has had a line of six live Bengal Tigers since the school raised $750 from its student body to purchase the first tiger from the Little Rock (Arkansas) Zoo in October 1936. All the Tigers have been nicknamed Mike in honor of former LSU athletic trainer Mike Chambers, who spearheaded the drive to purchase the first Mike. Mike the Tiger circles the Tiger Stadium playing field before every home game, strategically starting in the southeast corner that is the field entrance for visiting teams. After living in just a two thousand-square-foot caged area for years, Mike the Tiger moved into a $3 million, 15,000-square-foot habitat in 2005.

MIZZOU CONNECTION

Courtesy Mizzou Athletics Media Relations

All-time football record vs. Missouri: 0-1

1978: Missouri 20, LSU 15 (Liberty Bowl, Memphis)

After playing the nation's toughest schedule under first-year coach Warren Powers, Missouri ended a five-year bowl drought with a trip to Memphis to face LSU, led by Charles McClendon in his penultimate of eighteen seasons on the Tigers' sideline. Both teams featured a senior consensus All-American on offense—running back Charles Alexander for LSU, tight end Kellen Winslow for Mizzou—but Powers' Tigers had more firepower. Running back James Wilder ran for 115 yards and a touchdown, while Earl Gant added another 46 yards and a score. Quarterback Phil Bradley tossed a 16-yard touchdown to Winslow and outplayed both LSU quarterbacks, who combined to throw four interceptions.

Not so sweet for Stewart: College basketball coaching royalty collided in the Midwest region at the 1980 NCAA Tournament. Among the coaches in the region were Dean Smith, Denny Crum, Digger Phelps, Eddie Sutton, Jack Hartman . . . and LSU's Dale Brown and Missouri's Norm Stewart. Meeting in the Sweet Sixteen, Brown's top-seeded Tigers topped Stewart's fifth-seeded Tigers 68-63 in Houston, even though Missouri outshot and outrebounded Brown's team. LSU fell to eventual national champion Louisville in the regional final but reached the Final Four a year later, an accomplishment that eclipsed Stewart's otherwise brilliant Missouri career.

Cat fancy: The origin of both schools' Tiger nicknames come from opposite sides of the Civil War. The Missouri Tigers were a Union militia that banded together to guard Columbia and the MU campus from pro-Confederate guerrillas rumored to be headed for the area during the war. The Tigers safely protected Columbia as "Bloody" Bill Anderson and his marauders took another path, and years later, when it came time to give MU's football team a name, the school chose Tigers to recognize the town's protectors. Meanwhile, the Tiger Rifles were a voluntary company from New Orleans that fought for the Confederacy. Over time, all infantry troops from Louisiana who served under Robert E. Lee came to be known as Tigers. In 1896, the school adopted Fighting Tigers as a nickname for the football team. Unlike LSU, Missouri does not have a live tiger mascot on site, but in 1999 the school launched Mizzou Tigers for Tigers, the country's first mascot conservation program aimed at preserving tiger populations in the wild.

GAME DAY

MEDIA

Broadcasting the Game: WDGL-FM 98.1 in Baton Rouge is the flagship station; WWL-AM 870 in New Orleans

Covering the Tigers: www.theadvocate.com/sports/lsu/ (*The Advocate*, Baton Rouge), www.nola.com/lsu/ (*Times-Picayune*, New Orleans), www.tigerrag.com/ (*Tiger Rag Magazine*, Baton Rouge)

TAILGATING

Tailgating is not permitted on sidewalks, bike paths, and landscaped areas. The use of electrical outlets in or on LSU facilities or other utilities such as water sources is a strict no-no. Portable electrical generators are permitted, but also discouraged. Music must be confined to your tailgate area. All music must be shut off by midnight the night before games and by 2 a.m. after games. LSU discourages the use of tents larger than 10' x 10', and tents may not be staked into the ground. Tents may not be set up anywhere that impedes pedestrian traffic, and all tents should be taken down before entering the game.

SHUTTLE

For $20 per person per game, LSU has bus services from two places. The first location, with pickup four hours before kickoff, is the Westmoreland Shopping Center, near the intersection of South Acadian Thruway and Government Street. The second location, with pickup two hours before kickoff, is at Farr Park, south of the LSU campus on River Road for fans that park motor homes in that location. Buses for both locations will pick up post-game on North Stadium Drive. A limited number of shuttle passes are available for purchase on www.LSUtix.net beginning in early August.

TRADITIONS

Night games: LSU's passion for playing night home games in Tiger Stadium has never been better explained than by ESPN analyst Beano Cook who said, "Dracula and LSU football are at their best when the sun goes down." LSU has played night football for eighty years heading into the 2012 season and has a considerably better record in night games in the last five decades.

White jerseys: In 1958, then-Tigers coach Paul Dietzel decided that his team would wear white jerseys for every home game. That year, LSU won its first national title, and the white jerseys were considered good luck. The Tigers rarely donned their purple jerseys at home until the NCAA changed its jersey rule requiring home teams to wear dark jerseys. LSU was forced to wear purple jerseys for home games from 1983 to 1994. In 1995, then-new LSU coach Gerry DiNardo successfully petitioned the NCAA football rules committee to amend the rule to where the visiting team could give the home team permission to wear white. The SEC eventually adopted a rule saying the home team has first choice of jersey color.

B-BALL, ETC.

LSU is one of a handful of colleges that had three men's basketball players selected to the NBA's list of greatest fifty players ever—Bob Pettit, "Pistol" Pete Maravich, and Shaquille O'Neal. LSU's power sport shifted from men's and women's outdoor and indoor track and field (winning a combined thirty NCAA team championships between 1987 to 2008) to baseball, which won six College World Series between 1991 and 2009.

ABOUT TOWN

It seems like everybody has had a piece of Baton Rouge since French explorers founded it in 1699. The flags of France, England, Spain, West Florida, Louisiana, Confederate States of America, and the United States have flown over the city. Louisiana was admitted into the Union on April 8, 1812. Five years later, Baton Rouge (a French translation of the Indian term "red stick") was incorporated. The city became the state capital in 1849. The petrochemical industry bolstered more growth in the 1950s and 1960s. The city also experienced an unexpected temporary growth spurt in 2006 when 200,000 displaced Hurricane Katrina refugees fled to Baton Rouge from New Orleans and other affected areas.

LODGING

HIlton Capitol Center: Now in its third life, from the Heidelberg Hotel to the Capitol House Hotel and now to the Capitol Center, this Hilton is ten minutes north of Tiger Stadium in downtown Baton Rouge, overlooking the Mississippi River. *201 Lafayette St., Baton Rouge, LA 70801, 225-344-5866, www.hilton.com*

The Cook Hotel and Conference Center at LSU: Owned and operated by the LSU Alumni Association, this 128-room hotel and conference center has a nice view of the campus lakes. *3848 W. Lakeshore Dr., Baton Rouge, LA 70808, 225-383-2665, www.thecookhotel.com*

Renaissance Baton Rouge: A 256-room Marriott property that is Baton Rouge's newest luxury hotel. Located just off Interstate 10 at the edge of the Mall of Louisiana. *7000 Bluebonnet Blvd., Baton Rouge, LA 70810, 225-215-7000, www. marriott.com*

EATING

Mike Anderson's Seafood: Anderson, a former LSU All-American linebacker from the late 1960s, started his restaurant in the mid-1970s. Order "The Guitreau," grilled fish covered in a crawfish/crab/mushroom/onion white wine sauce. *1031 W. Lee Dr., Baton Rouge, LA 70809, 225-766-7823, www.mikeandersons.com*

Ruffino's: Chef Peter Sclafani III, the restaurant's co-owner along with former LSU lineman Ruffin Rodrigue, have a menu described as Creole-Italian. *18811 Highland Rd., Baton Rouge, LA 70809, 225-753-3458, www.ruffinosrestaurant.com*

Coffee Call: Open twenty-four hours a day, Coffee Call serves the breakfast nectar of South Louisiana, café au lait, and beignets. They have other menu items, but you'll never get to them once you've had the beignets. *3132 College Dr., Baton Rouge, LA 70808, 225-925-9493*

SIGHTSEEING

Louisiana State Capitol: With its 27th-floor observation deck 350 feet above the ground, the tallest state capitol building in the U.S. (34 floors, 450 feet high) has spectacular free-to-the-public views of downtown Baton Rouge and the Mississippi River. *900 North 3rd St., Baton Rouge, LA 70802, 225-342-7317*

The Myrtles Plantation: Get your Ghostbusters groove on by touring an Antebellum plantation more than 210 years old that is considered one of America's most haunted homes. Call or visit the website for tour times and admission prices. *7747 U.S. Highway 61, St. Francisville, LA 70775, 225-635-6277, www.myrtlesplantation.com*

Louisiana Art and Science Museum and Irene W. Pennington Planetarium: This place connects art and science to encourage discovery and creativity. The state-of-the-art planetarium is spectacular. Call or visit website for admission prices. *100 River Road South, Baton Rouge, LA 70802, 225-344-5272, www.lasm.org*

SHOPPING

Mall of Louisiana: A 1.6 million-square-foot, two-level enclosed mall with 175 retailers, including everything from an Apple Store to Williams Sonoma. Easily accessible to Interstate 10 and surrounded by restaurants like Louisiana-based Ralph and Kacoos, as well as Copeland's Cheesecake Bistro. *6401 Bluebonnet Blvd., Baton Rouge, LA 70836 225-761-7228, www.malloflouisiana.com*

Baton Rouge Arts Market: Artists from Louisiana and Mississippi who create pottery, jewelry, glass sculptures, textiles, photographs, woodwork, etc., gather on the first Saturday of each month (excluding January and May) from 8 a.m. until noon at 5th and Main streets in downtown Baton Rouge to sell their creations. *5th and Main Sts., Baton Rouge, LA 70802, 225-344-8558, www.artsbr.org*

Tanger Outlets: Twenty-five miles from Tiger Stadium east on Interstate 10 toward New Orleans at Exit 177, Tanger is a magnificent collection of outlet stores for almost every big-name brand imaginable—Coach, Guess, Nike, Tommy Hilfiger, Kenneth Cole, just to name a few. *2410 Tanger Blvd., Gonzales, LA 70737, 225-647-9383, www.tangeroutlet.com/gonzales*

NIGHTLIFE

The Varsity Theatre: It's an old theatre that has long since been a converted concert venue and a popular bar that's just steps away from LSU's north gate. On game days, management breaks out a huge big screen. *3353 Highland Rd., Baton Rouge, LA 70802, 225-383-7018, www.varsitytheatre.com*

Walk-Ons Bistreaux and Bar: Opened in 2003 by Jack Warner and Brandon Landry, a couple of former LSU basketball walk-ons from the late 1990s, this premier sports bar is walking distance (or stumbling, depending on your alcoholic intake) from Tiger Stadium. *3838 Burbank Dr., Baton Rouge, LA 70808, 225-757-8010, www.walk-ons.com*

The Roux House: Downtown Baton Rouge's party place with great drink specials, a lively crowd, and consistently excellent local bands like Beer for Breakfast. *143 3rd St., Baton Rouge, LA 70801, 225-344-2583, www.rouxhousebr.com*

TRAVELING TO BATON ROUGE?

It's a twelve-hour drive from Columbia to LSU's campus. On that note, flying looks like the better option. Fans can fly from St. Louis or Kansas City into Baton Rouge Metropolitan Airport with a stop in Atlanta, Houston, or Dallas. The Mizzou Alumni Association hosts a Tiger Tailgate. Visit MizzouSportsTravel.com for more information on tickets and pricing.

MISSISSIPPI STATE

The Agricultural and Mechanical College of the State of Mississippi—the original name of Mississippi State—would have been mighty difficult to fit on the name of a football jersey. It took just over fifty years after the school's doors first opened with eighty students in the fall of 1880 for the school be renamed Mississippi State College.

Two years before it opened, the university was created by the Mississippi Legislature on February 28, 1878, with the intent of opening a school that offered training in agriculture, horticulture, and the mechanical arts while not excluding other scientific and classical studies, including military tactics. Various pieces of federal legislation added elements to the campus, such as the creation of the Agricultural Experiment Station in 1888. Other key dates for the school were receiving its first accreditation by the Southern Association of Colleges and Schools (1926) and the school being re-named Mississippi State University (1958) by the state legislature.

Today, the university offers such diverse majors as PGA golf course management in its school

---

MISSISSIPPI STATE UNIVERSITY

Students: 20,424

Starkville: pop. 23,888

Davis Wade Stadium: seats 55,082

Colors: Maroon and White

Nickname: Bulldogs

Mascot: Bully

Campus Attractions: Colvard Student Union, MSU Institute of Golf

Phone: 662-325-2323 (general information)
662-325-2121 (campus police)
662-325-8082 (athletic department)

Tickets: 662-325-2600

---

of business. Naturally, State's campus golf course has been nominated by *Golfweek* and *Golf Digest* magazine as one of the premier public courses in the United States. It is as manicured and well-kept as Davis Wade Stadium, where State's football team has played since 1914 when it was known as Scott Field.

The school's football program got off to a snail's pace start. The sport was first played at the school then known as Mississippi A&M in intramural competition and some faculty-student games. W. M. Matthews of Harrisburg, Texas, an A&M agricultural student, is credited as organizing the first team in 1895. En route to the team's first game in Jackson, Tennessee, against Southwestern Baptist, Matthews was asked to choose the team colors and quickly responded, "Maroon and White." Picking the colors was the highlight of the school's first two seasons in which A&M went a collective 0-6 and was outscored 172-0.

After the 1896 season, A&M didn't field a team for the next four years, initially because of the 1897 yellow fever epidemic. Finally in 1901, school president Jack Hardy revived the program and hired player-coach J. B. Harvey from Georgetown College in Kentucky. In the second game that season, A&M played in-state rival the University of Mississippi for the first time. Not only did A&M's team score in a game for the first time, it won 17-0. The game was delayed over a debate by both teams questioning the eligibility of certain players on each side. The delay resulted in the second half being shortened to six minutes because of darkness.

Afterwards, both schools insulted each other in campus publications. The A&M student newspaper wrote, "The University (of Mississippi) boys played the dirtiest game of ball we have seen." The *University of Mississippi Magazine* fired back, "To one who has never indulged in an exercise more violent than the milking of a patient cow, football seems a brutal sport."

Ironically, Mississippi State won its first SEC championship before Ole Miss, going 8-1-1 and 4-0-1 to win the league title in 1941. It wrapped up the season

PROGRAM HIGHLIGHTS

NATIONAL CHAMPIONSHIPS (0):

SEC CHAMPIONSHIPS (1): 1941

BOWL RECORD: 9-6 (.600). Last bowl—23-17 over Wake Forest in 2011 Music City Bowl

LONGEST WINNING STREAK: 13 games, 1942-44

WINNINGEST COACH: Jackie Sherrill (1991-2002), 75-75-2 (.500)

HEISMAN TROPHY WINNERS OR HIGHEST HEISMAN FINISH: Back Tom "Shorty" McWilliams, 10th in 1944

with a win at San Francisco on December 6, the day before the Japanese bombed Pearl Harbor. Unfortunately for Mississippi State, they have never again won an SEC football title. Though they have had some fine individual players over the years and are entering the 2012 season having won bowl games in consecutive seasons for just the second time in history, they are still chasing that elusive league championship. The closest they have been was in 1998 under Coach Jackie Sherrill when State led No. 1 ranked Tennessee, 14-10, with 8:43 left to play in the SEC championship game before losing 24-14 to the eventual national champions.

LEGENDS

Rockey Felker

The league's Player of the Year in 1974 as an MSU quarterback, Felker returned to his alma mater as head coach in 1986 and was fired after five years, and then came back to his school again in 2001 where he has been on the staff in some capacity ever since. He has been called "the greatest ambassador that Mississippi State has ever had."

D.D. Lewis

All-American linebacker at MSU from 1965 to 1967, Lewis was a tackling machine who went on to play in five Super Bowls in his thirteen-year NFL career with the Dallas Cowboys.

Jackie Parker

A junior college transfer who played just two years for the Bulldogs in 1952-53, Parker was named the SEC's Most Valuable Player both years. He once accounted for forty-two points in a game against Auburn, running and throwing for six touchdowns.

Jack Cristil

State's legendary play-by-play announcer for an incredible fifty-eight seasons, retiring in the spring of 2010, Cristil's signature call was "Wrap it in Maroon and White!" when the Bulldogs had a victory in hand.

NOTABLE ALUMS

George Bryan—Vice president of Sarah Lee Corporation

John Grisham—Best-selling author of legal thrillers

Marsha Blackburn—U.S. representative for Tennessee's 7th congressional district since 2003

Jerry Clower—Died in 1998 but is still considered the best-ever Southern-based country comedian

STADIUM

Davis Wade Stadium: Built in 1914 as Scott Field and named for Don Magruder Scott, one of Mississippi State's first football stars and an Olympic sprinter, Davis Wade Stadium is the second oldest football stadium in NCAA Division I-FBS. It has undergone four renovations and expansions (another one is planned) to raise capacity to 55,082. While it is just the second smallest stadium in the fourteen-team SEC, it has the league's largest and college football's third biggest high definition video replay board. The board is so mammoth and because the stadium size doesn't quite match it, it's like putting a one hundred-inch flat screen in a doublewide trailer.

MASCOTS

Mississippi State has an American Kennel Club–registered English Bulldog named "Bully" as a mascot. The school has had nicknames of Aggies and Maroons, and officially became Bulldogs in 1961. But the nickname Bulldogs had been used as far back as 1905 when then-Mississippi A&M's team was complimented for its "bulldog-style of play" in an 11-0 victory over Ole Miss. The school's first live game mascot came in 1935 when it obtained a bulldog named Ptolemy. One of Ptolemy's litter, named Bully, became mascot shortly thereafter but was killed in 1939 by a campus school bus. After a half-mile funeral procession featuring the school band and three ROTC battalions, the first Bully was buried under the bench at the fifty-yard line in Scott Field. Early Bullies lived in frat houses or wandered freely, but now Bully resides at the school's College of Veterinary Medicine.

MIZZOU CONNECTION

Courtesy Mizzou Athletics Media Relations

All-time football record vs. Missouri: 0-2

1981: Missouri 14, Mississippi State 3 (Jackson)

1984: Missouri 47, Mississippi State 30 (Columbia)

For years, Missouri had earned a reputation for slaying formidable foes away from home, and there was no shortage of confidence in 1981 when Warren Powers' 3-0 Tigers headed south to face the ninth-ranked Bulldogs. Emory Bellard, credited decades earlier for inventing Texas' wishbone offense, installed a new version at Mississippi State, the wingbone. But the Bulldogs were helpless against a Missouri attack led by Bobby Meyer, who ran for 122 yards and scored both touchdowns. Three years later, the teams combined for 978 yards of offense and the difference for Missouri was a 6-0 advantage in the turnover ratio.

Craving a slice: It's not uncommon for football staffs to trade secrets in the offseason, and that's what Dan Mullen was doing in Columbia in March 2008. Mullen, then Florida's offensive coordinator, was a year away from becoming Mississippi State's head coach. He was in town to study the nuances of Missouri's no-huddle spread offense. It wasn't his first stop in Columbia. Mullen was on the opposing sideline for Gary Pinkel's first game as Missouri's head coach in 2001, a stunning loss to Bowling Green. Mullen was the Falcons' quarterbacks coach. Mullen has admitted a soft spot for Columbia's popular eatery, Shakespeare's Pizza.

Cashing in: Since 1980, the Blue Note has treated music fans to countless concerts in Columbia. The most memorable came on April 22, 1994. That night, Johnny Cash, sixty-two at the time, brought down a packed house, playing his classics alongside wife June Carter, including "Folsom Prison Blues," "Ring of Fire," and "I Walk the Line." Three decades earlier, Cash was famously arrested in another college town, Starkville, Mississippi, where he was jailed overnight for public drunkenness. (Cash claimed he was picking flowers.) The incident later inspired his song "Starkville City Jail," and much later, the Johnny Cash Flower Pickin' Festival in Starkville. By all accounts, Cash was on his best behavior in Columbia, and the show still stands as the all-time favorite of the Blue Note's owner, Richard King.

GAME DAY

MEDIA

Broadcasting the Game: WZNO-FM (105.9) in Jackson, WXMX-FM (96.3) in Tupelo

Covering the Bulldogs: www.clarionledger.com/section/SPORTS030102/MSU-Mississippi-State-sports (*Jackson Clarion-Ledger*), www.commercialappeal.com (*Memphis Commercial Appeal*), www.nems360.com/pages/insidemississippistatesports (*Northeast Mississippi Daily Journal* in Tupelo), www.mississippistate.scout.com (Gene's Page)

TAILGATING

Almost all of the campus tailgating is confined to an area called the Junction, which is outside the south end of Davis Wade Stadium where Stone and Lee boulevards meet. The area is anchored by the stadium, Barnes & Noble bookstore, and the University Welcome Center. All tailgating areas open at 5 p.m. the day before the game, close at midnight daily, and must be vacated by 7 a.m. the day after the game. Small tents are permitted, but large tents that require stakes must be rented from MSU Event Services, 662-325-3228. Connection to university utilities is prohibited. Generators and charcoal grills are allowed, but charcoal must be disposed of responsibly.

SHUTTLE

Shuttles are available from downtown Starkville and the Thad Cochran Research, Technology and Economic Development Park just across Highway 182 on the edge of the MSU campus. The shuttles begin three hours prior to kickoff.

TRADITIONS

Cowbells: Whether cowbells have been legal or not—and the SEC legalized the ringing of cowbells two years ago before the 2010 season, thirty-six years after the SEC passed a rule banning artificial noisemakers—Mississippi State fans have clanged their beloved cowbells. The widely accepted origin of cowbells at Mississippi State happened in the 1930s when a Jersey cow wandered on the field at State's home game against Ole Miss. State won big that day, and its students immediately considered the cow a good luck charm. In the 1960s, Mississippi State professors Earl W. Terrell and Ralph L. Reeves came up with the idea of welding handles on the cowbells. Now, the SEC allows Bulldogs fans to ring cowbells at home games when there's not a live play. Current athletic director Scott Stricklin helped create the "Ring Responsibly" campaign aimed at educating fans when it is legal to ring. "We all have to learn this rule to do it the right way, because cowbells are part of who we are as an institution," Stricklin said. Even with the new rule, the SEC has fined State for ringing during live play.

Egg Bowl: Also known as the Battle of the Golden Egg, it's Mississippi State's annual game against in-state rival Ole Miss. The trophy awarded to the winner is retained by the winning team, until it loses an Egg Bowl.

B-BALL, ETC.

For an athletic program that traditionally has one of the lowest budgets in the league, Mississippi State has done surprisingly well. It's just one of five SEC schools—the others are Arkansas, Florida, Georgia, and LSU—that have played in a New Year's Day bowl in football, in the men's Final Four in basketball, and in the men's College World Series in baseball. Though the Bulldogs have never won a national championship in baseball, former MSU coach Ron Polk won 1,139 games guiding State, more victories than any SEC coach in any SEC sport in history. Polk is called "The Father of SEC Baseball" for his coaching and promotional skills advancing a sport that had previously been an afterthought in the SEC.

ABOUT TOWN

Evidence such as artwork and claypot fragments indicate Starkville has been inhabited since before the 1800s. White settlers were able to move to Starkville after the Treaty of Dancing Rabbit Creek in 1830. In the treaty, Choctaw Indian inhabitants of Oktibbeha County surrendered their claims to the land, which had two large springs. The town was first known as Boardtown, because of mill manufacturing clapboards southwest of town. But in 1835 when Boardtown was designated the county seat of Oktibbeha County, the name of the town was changed to Starkville in honor of General John Stark, who was a Revolutionary War hero.

LODGING

Historic Hotel Chester: Chester's thirty-seven rooms and suites are located in the heart of downtown Starkville. If you want a treat, wander a couple of doors down to Starkville Café and see what the locals are debating over breakfast. *101 N. Jackson St., Starkville, MS 39759, 662-323-5005, www.historichotelchester.com*

The Cedars Bed and Breakfast: There are four uniquely appointed bedrooms in this 1836 Antebellum mansion overlooking 183 acres of beautiful rolling hills and ponds. *2173 Oktoc Rd., Starkville, MS 39759, 662-324-7569*

Hilton Garden Inn: If you want new, the HGI has been open for business just a couple of years. It's two minutes tops to the MSU campus. *975 Highway 12 East, Starkville, MS 39759, 662-615-9664, www.hiltongardeninn.hilton.com*

EATING

The Veranda: Starkville's No. 1 restaurant serves up anything from pork chops and cream gravy (which is like a blood transfusion to a Southerner) to crawfish nachos. *208 Lincoln Green, Starkville, MS 39759, 662-323-1231, www.verandastarkville.com*

The Little Dooey: A gotta-eat-at this barbeque stop for almost any celeb that wanders through Starkville. *100 Fellowship St., Starkville, MS 39759, 662-323-6094, www.littledooey.com*

Cappe's Steakhouse: Amazing angus beef steaks, grilled over charcoal, served with all the trimmings. *105 Eckford Dr., Starkville, MS 39759, 662-324-1987, www.cappessteakhouse.com*

SIGHTSEEING

Peeples Pecan Company: Purchase or pick your own Mississippi-grown pecans at this local family's farm. Usually doesn't open for picking until November 1. *754 Pecan Dr., Starkville, MS 39759, 662-323-7038*

John Grisham Room: Located on the third floor of the Mitchell Memorial Library on the Mississippi State campus, this rotating exhibits shows examples of the popular author's (a Mississippi State and Ole Miss grad) creative process. *library.msstate.edu/grishamroom/*

Oktibbeha County Lake: If you love the great outdoors, it doesn't get any better than this 477-acre lake and the land surrounding it. *1505 Eastover Dr., Starkville, MS 39759, 662-323-3350, www.mdwfp.com*

SHOPPING

Aspen Bay Candle Company: Very cool place to tour and watch how these unique candles are handmade. Then you can go to the retail store and buy them. *Factory is at 1010 Lynn Lane, Starkville. Retail store is at 500 Russell St. (Cotton Crossing Shopping Center), Starkville, MS 39759, 662-323-0929, www. aspenbaycandles.com*

Smith and Byars: Businesses have come and gone on Main Street in Starkville, but this classic men's clothier has been in business since 1944. *122 E. Main St., Starkville, MS 39759, 662-323-5793*

Dandy Doodlez: A paint-your-own-pottery studio and gift shop located in downtown Starkville, you'll have a blast creating your own piece of pottery from a selection of over five hundred bisque shapes and more than fifty mosaic templates. *222 East Main St., Starkville, MS 39759, 662-324-1880, www. dandydoodlez.com*

NIGHTLIFE

Rick's Café: It's two clubs in one. Rick's Café is located in the back and is a concert venue open every Friday and Saturday and during the week for special shows. In the front of the building is the Blue Parrot Sports Pub, open seven days a week. *319B Highway 182 East, Starkville, MS 39759, 662-323-7425, www. rickscafe.net*

Cowbell's: Voted the No. 1 nightclub in Starkville by readers of the *Starkville Daily News*, this place has a steady lineup of live music, even if you never heard of most of the acts like DJ Bizzle or The Spunk Monkees (but these Tupelo boys do rock!). *1545 St. Andrews Ln., Starkville, MS 39759, 662-615-9600, www. cowbellssportsgrill.com*

Mugshots Grill and Bar: This sports bar has an exceptionally extensive menu of dishes named for friends and family members (Rajun "Hester" Cajun Chicken Salad) of the creator's of this Hattiesburg-based franchise. The hamburgers are awesome. *101 N. Douglas Conner Dr., Starkville, MS 39759, 662-324-3965, www.mugshotsgrillandbar.com*

TRAVELING TO STARKVILLE?

It's at least a nine-hour drive from Columbia to MSU's campus. I-55 will take you from St. Louis to Memphis, and from there it's another three hours to Starkville, either through Tupelo or Oxford. The nearest airport is Golden Triangle Regional, which offers daily connectors to Memphis. The Mizzou Alumni Association hosts a Tiger Tailgate. Visit MizzouSportsTravel.com for more information on tickets and pricing.

MISSOURI

With a winning offer of $117,900, Boone County outbid five other mid-Missouri counties in June 1839 to be unanimously awarded the location of the land-grant state university. Four years later, as the nation celebrated its birthday on July 4, 1843, the university, the first of its kind west of the Mississippi River, formally celebrated its dedication. "Singularly auspicious to the occasion, the morning was ushered in by as bright a sun as ever shed radiance from a cloudless sky," wrote the next day's *Columbia Statesman*.

Over time, Columbia and the state's flagship university grew in size, and by the close of the century its appetite for football was born. In 1890, Austin Lee McRae, an assistant professor of physics at what was then called Missouri State University visited St. Louis where he stumbled on a group of students at Washington University playing football, a game he had dabbled in while a student at Harvard. McRae returned to Columbia and scrambled together a team of students and arranged a game against the team from St. Louis. Among the nineteen players on McRae's team were eight law students, including William Littell, the captain and center; Dennis Kane, the quarterback; and Charles Keith, a

UNIVERSITY OF MISSOURI

Students: 33,805

Columbia: pop. 108,500

Memorial Stadium: seats 71,004

Colors: Black and Gold

Nickname: Tigers

Mascot: Truman the Tiger

Campus Attractions: The Columns, George Caleb Bingham Gallery, Museum of Art and Archeology, Reynolds Journalism Institute

Phone: 573-882-2121 (general information)
573-882-7201 (campus police)
573-882-6501 (athletic department)

Tickets: 573-884-PAWS or www.mutigers.com

halfback who became the first player to score a touchdown in the program's first official game.

After his return from St. Louis, McRae and eleven of the students met on October 10 and discussed forming an athletic association for the university. The group soon hit its first obstacle. The 1892 edition of *The Savitar* recapped that meeting: "Owing to the lack of funds and to the general apathy in regard to athletics among the students, it would be impossible to form a general athletic association at that time but that a special effort be made to organize a football team to form the nucleus of a future athletic association."

The football pioneers, as they've since been hailed, carried on with plans to form a team, and up first was a scrimmage against other MSU students, forever known in the annals of Mizzou history as Picked Team. McRae's players outscored Picked Team 22-6 on October 20. A month later, McRae took his band of footballers to St. Louis, where they wore knit caps of black and gold—team colors picked by McRae—and were squashed by Wash U. 28-0 on Thanksgiving Day.

Years later, the night before the 1922 season finale against Kansas, the fullback from Missouri's inaugural team, Burton Thompson, gave a speech on campus and recalled that Thanksgiving Day shellacking. The speech was transcribed in the *Missouri Alumnus* magazine: "They had won a victory, but we were not defeated and that is the spirit that lives and inspires and wins for the Tigers today."

Missouri closed its first season of organized football with a 90-0 smashing of Engineers Eleven, giving MSU a 2-1 record for the year. By the next fall, McRae had left for a faculty position at the University of Texas, but his legacy survived. "It was he who inspired and encouraged us to our first efforts at football," Thompson said thirty-two years later, "which if somewhat unseasonable were none the less fruitful of good results."

PROGRAM HIGHLIGHTS

MISSOURI VALLEY CONFERENCE CHAMPIONSHIPS (6): 1909, 1913, 1919, 1924, 1925, 1927

BIG SIX CHAMPIONSHIPS (4): 1939, 1941, 1942, 1945

BIG EIGHT CHAMPIONSHIPS (2): 1960, 1969

BIG 12 CHAMPIONSHIPS (0): Mizzou won the North Division twice in 2007 and 2008

BOWL RECORD: 13-16 (.448). Last bowl—41-24 over North Carolina in 2011 Independence Bowl

LONGEST WINNING STREAK: 12 games, 1959-60

WINNINGEST COACH: Don Faurot (1935-42, 1946-56), 101-79-10, 55.8 percent

HEISMAN TROPHY WINNERS OR HIGHEST HEISMAN FINISH: Quarterback Paul Christman, 1939, third place

Over the next forty-four years, twenty different men would coach the program as Missouri captured six Missouri Valley Conference championships but fell on hard times, competitively and financially, in the 1930s. Former Tiger player Don Faurot, the pride of Mountain Grove, Missouri, who wasn't naïve to the instability his alma mater had endured, came to the rescue. "I don't know one thing, not a single thing, more overconfident than for a Missouri football coach to buy a house," Faurot said at one of his early press conferences in 1935, Bob Broeg later wrote in *Ol' Mizzou: A Century of Tiger Football*. But the volatility at the top ended under Faurot, who coached Mizzou to 101 wins over 19 seasons, ushering the program out of debt and into the national spotlight.

LEGENDS

Don Faurot

A former Tiger halfback, Faurot stabilized the program as coach and AD coming out of the Great Depression. He invented the Split-T formation, which introduced option football to college offenses and helped spawn the wishbone and veer attacks. The namesake of Missouri's field, Faurot oversaw tremendous growth within the program and athletic department and in 1961 was inducted in the National Football Foundation Hall of Fame.

Paul Christman

A genuine dual-threat quarterback, "Pitchin' Paul" won twenty of his twenty-eight starts from 1938 to 1940 and held most school passing records for almost forty years. In 1956, he became Missouri's first player inducted in the NFF Hall of Fame. His No. 44 is one of seven retired Missouri jerseys.

Dan Devine

Devine oversaw the most successful era of Mizzou football as the Tigers finished in the top twenty nine times during his thirteen seasons. His punishing defenses allowed just 9.6 points per game during the 1960s and posted twenty-seven shutouts. He joined Faurot in the Hall of Fame in 1985.

Roger Wehrli

A brilliant cornerback and return specialist, the King City, Missouri, native was an All-American in 1968 when he picked off seven passes and led the country in punt return yardage. He's one of just two Tigers enshrined in both the college and pro halls of fame.

Among Faurot's many achievements was building a program capable of attracting star power in his wake. That's what he did as athletic director in 1958, landing up-and-coming Arizona State coach Dan Devine, who oversaw the Tigers for thirteen seasons, including a remarkable run during the 1960s, when Mizzou won 76.2 percent of its games.

The program had its moments of glory in the 1970s, 1980s, and 1990s and its share of struggle and heartbreak, none more agonizing than the infamous "Fifth Down" against Colorado in 1990 and the "Flea Kicker" against Nebraska in 1997. Mizzou finally began to experience sustained success when Gary Pinkel arrived in 2001 as the Tigers won back-to-back Big 12 North Division titles, spent a week at No. 1 in the polls in 2007, averaged ten wins from 2007 to 2010, and played in a school-record seven consecutive bowl games. Heading into the 2012 season, Pinkel's program was one of only six among the major conferences to win at least eight games each of the past six seasons, joining LSU, Oklahoma, USC, Virginia Tech, and West Virginia.

Kellen Winslow
In the NFL, Winslow helped revolutionize the tight end position but first honed his pass-catching prowess with the Tigers, earning All-American honors his senior year. Like Wehrli, he's a member of both the college and pro halls of fame.

Chase Daniel
The triggerman in Mizzou's prolific spread offense, Daniel holds every significant school passing record after winning thirty games in three seasons as a starter. Voted the 2007 Big 12 athlete of the year, Daniel finished fourth in the Heisman voting that season after guiding MU to the No. 1 ranking for one week.

MASCOT

To protect Columbia from a rumored band of marauders under the leadership of notorious hell-raiser "Bloody" Bill Anderson, Columbia citizens formed an armed guard in the fall of 1864 and built a blockhouse at Broadway and 8th Street to protect the downtown courthouse. They called themselves the Missouri Tigers. Word must have spread, because Anderson took a detour around Columbia and left the town unmolested. Shortly after the university's football team was born, Tigers was suggested and approved as the team nickname, a tribute to the citizens who kept the town alive.

For years, a generic tiger stood as the school mascot, but he was given a name in 1984—Truman, for Missouri native and former president Harry Truman. In 1986, MU debuted a new and improved Truman at the season-opening football game against Utah State. Since then, Truman has been a fixture on the sidelines and gets into occasional mischief. He made national headlines at the 2011 Independence Bowl when he picked up and dropped the crystal trophy, shattering the award a few hours before kickoff. He had no comment.

FIGHT SONG

"FIGHT TIGER"

Fight, Tiger, fight for old Mizzou,

Right behind you, everyone is with you.

Break the line and follow down the field,

And, you'll be, on the top, upon the top.

Fight, Tiger, you will always win,

Proudly keep the colors flying skyward.

In the end, we'll win the victory,

So Tiger, fight for Old Mizzou!

STADIUM

Memorial: Dedicated in 1926 in honor of 113 Missouri grads and students who died in World War I, the Tigers' home has undergone significant growth over time. Known for its collection of painted white rocks aligned in the shape of an M behind the north end zone, Memorial Stadium has gone from natural grass to OmniTurf to grass and again to FieldTurf. In 1972, the playing surface was named Faurot Field, in honor of longtime coach and athletic director Don Faurot. Penn State drew the stadium's biggest crowd (75,298) in 1980, but MU has since reduced the capacity to 71,004.

Courtesy Mizzou Athletics Media Relations

NOTABLE ALUMS

Chris Cooper—Oscar-winning actor

Sheryl Crow—Singer and musician

Jon Hamm—Actor, star of *Mad Men*

Mort Walker—Cartoonist, "Beetle Bailey"

Sam Walton—Wal-Mart co-founder

GAME DAY

MEDIA

Broadcasting the Game: Tiger Radio Network throughout the state, including KCMQ-FM 96.7 and KTGR-AM 1580 in Columbia

Covering the Tigers: www.TigerExtra.com (*Columbia Daily Tribune*), www.columbiamissourian.com (*Columbia Missourian*), www.kansascity.com (*Kansas City Star*), www.stltoday.com (*St. Louis Post-Dispatch*), www.PowerMizzou.com (Rivals.com affiliate)

TAILGATING

Fans flock to the parking lots around Memorial Stadium for tailgating, from the prime spots in Lots A, C, and D near the stadium to Reactor Field south of Mizzou Arena on the west side of Providence Road. Alcoholic drinks may be served in such areas, though excessive quantities of alcohol are not allowed in vehicles or in the parking lots.

Tents should not exceed 10' x 10' and should be placed immediately in front of or behind your vehicle. Also, tents are only allowed in parking lots and adjacent grass areas for those with parking passes in those respective lots. Parking spaces and tent locations are first-come, first-served for those holding proper parking pass hangtags in each lot once the lots open on game days. MizzouTailgating.com will answer all your game-day tailgating questions.

SHUTTLE

Courtesy Shuttles are available from each lot to the south and east of Memorial Stadium to designated points around the stadium. The service operates ninety minutes before and one hour after the game. Accessible shuttles will operate between the Hearnes Center accessible parking area and Gate 1. Pregame shuttles are also available from Lot U and Lot X to Gate 1. Lot U and Lot X shuttles only operate before the game and not after. MizzouGameDay.com will answer any questions and update any policy changes.

The city of Columbia also offers stadium shuttle service with four different routes, stopping at most hotels around town and various downtown locations. Cost is $1.50 each way per person. For more information visit www.gocolumbiamo.com or call 573-874-7282.

TRADITIONS

Marching Mizzou: With 310 members, the school's marching band is the largest student organization on campus and sets the tone for MU's game-day environment. "The Missouri Waltz," the official state song and a traditional part of the game-day regimen, should fit right into the SEC with these lyrics: "Hush-a-bye ma baby, go to sleep on Mammy's knee. Journey back to Dixieland in dreams again with me. . . ." Under band director Brad Snow, Marching Mizzou plays a unique arrangement of the familiar tune. "The slower traditional opening section gives fans a chance to wave their hands until the 'cut time' faster section," Snow said. "During this section they clap their hands and cheer loudly during the chant section. Go! Fight! Win! Tigers!"

Rock M: In 1927, the freshman class took stones left over from Memorial Stadium's construction and arranged them in the shape of an M on the hill behind the north end zone, an unmistakably unique symbol that measures 90 feet wide by 95 feet long. Every August, students slap on a new coat of white paint, sometimes while the football team holds a preseason practice just a few feet away. "What loyal Missourian can behold that stone 'M' without experiencing a queer tingling in the blood?" wrote *The Savitar* in 1930.

Adios, goalposts: After significant upsets on Faurot Field, it's become tradition for fans to topple the goalposts and lug them approximately 1.5 miles to Harpo's Bar and Grill (29 S. 10th St.), a ritual that is believed to have started in the early 1970s. Miraculously, a hacksaw always appears when the goalposts arrive, and fans take turns slicing the goalposts into instant chunks of memorabilia. The ritual last occurred October 23, 2010, when the Tigers upset top-ranked Oklahoma.

LAST-MINUTE TIPS

Where to Shop: The District is home to 110 unique shops and more than 70 restaurants with plenty of stops to buy game-day gear, including Jock's Nitch (16 S. 9th St.).

Where to Buy Tickets: In an online poll of Mizzou fans, most preferred www.StubHub.com (415-222-8400) as their choice for online ticket brokers, though others preferred www.FanSnap.com (650-645-4700), www.GoTickets.com (1-800-775-1617), and www.TheTicketGuys.com (877-877-4849).

B-BALL, ETC.

With a stunning first-round exit in the 2012 NCAA Tournament, Missouri's men's college basketball program continues to hold the dubious distinction of making the second-most NCAA appearances (25) without reaching the Final Four. Sixteen of those appearances came under Norm Stewart, a standout baseball and basketball player for the Tigers in the 1950s whose head-coaching career at Mizzou spanned four decades. Despite the tournament shortcomings, the Tigers have won fifteen regular-season league championships and reached the Elite Eight four times since 1976. Mizzou has produced twenty All-Americans and thirteen first-round NBA draft picks, including Keyon Dooling (No. 10, 2000), Doug Smith (No. 5, 1991), and Steve Stipanovich (No. 2, 1983). After Stewart retired in 1999, MU endured the tumultuous Quin Snyder era and a brief rebirth under Mike Anderson before he left for Arkansas. In 2011, Missouri officials were widely lampooned for hiring Miami's Frank Haith, but in his first campaign, the Tigers set a school record with twenty-seven regular-season victories, captured the Big 12 Tournament, and Haith was voted AP National Coach of the Year.

ABOUT TOWN

Columbia prides itself on its college-town atmosphere mixed with a big-city embrace of arts, education, and business. Higher education is the trade of the town as Mizzou shares the city limits with Columbia College and Stephens College, though health care and insurance are also staples of the local economy. Columbia's entertainment scene has thrived as well, putting itself on the map nationally with the Roots N Blues N BBQ Festival and True/False Film Fest. In the 2010 census, Columbia ranked fifth in population among Missouri cities, trailing only Kansas City, St. Louis, Springfield, and Independence.

LODGING

Holiday Inn Executive Center: Just off I-70 and across from the Columbia Mall, this hotel has three hundred rooms, including ten luxury suites, plus two restaurants: Churchill's, featuring some of Columbia's finest up-scale dining, and Sports Zone Restaurant & Grill, home to more than thirty flat-screen plasma TVs. *2200 I-70 Drive SW, Columbia, MO 65203, 573-445-8531, www. holidaycolumbia.com*

Stoney Creek Inn & Conference Center: Stay in one of 180 outdoorsy themed rooms, have a drink at Antler's Bar or take a dip in the Wilderness Park Pool—all just a mile south of Memorial Stadium. *2601 S. Providence Rd., Columbia, MO 65203, 573-442-6400*

Columbia's hotels fill up fast, but fans can also try nearby towns Jefferson City, Kingdom City, and Boonville, home of the Isle of Capri Casino & Hotel (660-882-1200).

EATING

Shakespeare's Pizza: Named in 2011 by *Good Morning America* as America's favorite college hangout, the downtown pizzeria is regularly packed with students, families, and visiting alums. Open since 1973, the restaurant lives by its mission statement: "It's the pizza, stupid. And maybe the beer. Everything else can go fly. Have a good time doing it, just wash your hands before and after." *225 S. 9th St., Columbia, MO 65201, 573-449-2454, www.shakespeares.com*

CJ's: A regular stop for a pregame or postgame helping of the hottest wings in town, this locally owned downtown restaurant smothers its signature dish in BYFO sauce: Burn Your Face Off. And they will. *704 E. Broadway, Columbia, MO 65201, 573-442-7777, www.cjsintigercountry.com*

Booches Billiard Hall: Served up on a piece of wax paper, Booches' slider-style burgers are the juiciest of Columbia's guilty pleasures. Hit the ATM on your way in because only cash is accepted at this no-frills eatery. *110 S. 9th St., Columbia, MO 65201, 573-874-9519*

Courtesy Mizzou Athletics Media Relations

SIGHTSEEING

Rock Bridge Memorial State Park: Open all year from dawn to dusk, the 2,273-acre park features a rock bridge formation, sinkholes, hiking and biking trails, and picnic area in the Gans Creek Wild Area. For courageous explorers, take a tour through the Devil's Icebox Cave, a seven-mile underground passage. *5901 South Highway 163, Columbia, MO 65203, 573-449-7402, www.mostateparks. com/park/rock-bridge-memorial-state-park*

Les Bourgeois Vineyards: The family-owned-and-operated vineyard features a blufftop view of the Missouri River Valley and offers outdoor picnic dining or an indoor bistro, plus its collection of ten locally made red and white wines. Located just twelve miles west of Columbia in Rocheport. *14020 W. Highway BB, Rocheport, MO 65279, 800-690-1830, www.missouriwine.com*

SHOPPING

The Shoppes At Stadium: You'll find a wide variety of clothing options in this collection of stores, from Old Navy to Macy's to Dick's Sporting Goods to Alumni Hall, which specializes in Mizzou gear. *Intersection of W. Ash St. & N. Stadium Blvd., Columbia, MO 65203*

Tiger Spirit: A fixture on 9th Street in the District since the 1980s, this one-stop shop for officially licensed Mizzou gear offers the latest in T-shirts, jerseys, sweatshirts, hats, kids clothes, banners, flags, and souvenirs. *111 S. 9th St., Columbia, MO 65201, www.tigerspirit.com*

NIGHTLIFE

Shiloh Bar & Grill: Located in the old Katy Station depot, Shiloh and its extended patio offer a great pregame and postgame spot for drinks, food, and live music. *402 E. Broadway, Columbia, MO 65201, 573-875-1800, www.shilohbar.com*

Déjà Vu: Established in 1975, the Vu is Columbia's home for stand-up comedy and features a massive 10,000-square-foot night club with a dance floor hailed as the city's best by *Inside Columbia Magazine*. *405 Cherry St., Columbia, MO 65201, 573-443-3216, www.dejavucomedy.com*

Harpo's Bar & Grill: Regularly voted one of America's best college bars, this downtown landmark has been serving cold drinks to Tiger fans since 1971. From the rooftop Skyy Bar to 10 Below, the West Coast-inspired night club located in the basement, there's more than one way to celebrate the night at the corner of 10th and Cherry. *29 S. 10th St., Columbia, MO 65201, 573-443-5418, www.harposcomo.com*

TRAVELING TO COLUMBIA?

Columbia is smack dab in the middle of Missouri and most easily accessible by Interstate 70 from the east or west or Highways 63 and 54 from the north and south. Columbia Regional Airport offers direct flights to Memphis and, starting in June 2012, a direct flight to and from Atlanta.

OLE MISS

Every day, University of Mississippi students pass by The Lyceum, which houses the school's administrative offices. The Lyceum was built in 1848 when the school opened for business with eighty students and six buildings on its campus. The Lyceum had all the classrooms and faculty offices. Fast forward to the Civil War in 1861 and The Lyceum became a hospital for both Confederate and Union soldiers. Two hundred fifty soldiers who died in the hospital were buried in a campus cemetery.

Move on 101 years and The Lyceum was at the heart of civil rights riots that took place when James Meredith, an African-American U.S. Air Force veteran, won a lawsuit that allowed him to integrate the all-white school. Meredith was blocked three times in September 1962 from entering the campus to enroll by then Mississippi governor Ross Barnett. On his fourth try, and escorted by U.S. marshals, Meredith entered the campus on September 30, 1962. Riots broke out between protesting segregationists and a combination of U.S. marshals and the national guardsmen. Two people died during the riots, including a French journalist, and more than two hundred marshals and guardsmen were injured.

UNIVERSITY OF MISSISSIPPI

Students: 20,844

Oxford: pop. 16,586

Vaught-Hemingway Stadium: seats 60,580

Colors: Red and Blue

Nickname: Rebels

Mascot: Black Bear

Campus Attractions: The Grove, The Lyceum

Phone: 662-915-7211 (general information)
662-915-4911 (campus police for emergencies)
662-915-7241 (athletic department)

Tickets: 662-915-7167

It's ironic that the riots took place at the height of Ole Miss's football glory. Though the program began 1893, started by a school professor named Alexander Lee Bondurant, it didn't make its mark until 1947 when the school hired John Howard Vaught as its head coach.

Vaught, a former TCU All-American, had been at Ole Miss (a name taken from the school's first yearbook in 1897) just one season in 1946 under Red Drew, an Alabama assistant. When the Rebels went 2-7 that season and Alabama head coach Frank Thomas resigned due to illness, Drew returned to Tuscaloosa to fill his spot. That left the Ole Miss vacancy for Vaught, and it was the greatest hire the school has ever made. In his very first year as head coach, the Rebels won their first SEC championship. Making in-state recruiting a priority and using a rollout passing attack that stymied many colleges, Vaught and the Rebels eventually enjoyed the best stretch of football in the school's history from 1957 to 1963. In those seven years, Ole Miss was 64-7-7, winning three SEC championships and a Football Writers Association of America national championship.

Since then, despite having some outstanding players like the father-son quarterbacking duo of Archie and Eli Manning about thirty years apart, the Rebels haven't won an SEC title since 1963. They are the only Western Division SEC school that has never qualified to play in the league championship game that originated in 1992.

Like the rest of the SEC, the Rebels didn't recruit their first African-American player until the early 1970s when Ben Williams and James Reed became the first black signees on December 11, 1971.

Ole Miss coaches that preceded Vaught complained for years that the school's segregationist past was being used against the Rebels in athletic recruiting. That's why recent Ole Miss administrations, despite getting heat from traditionalists, have taken measures to sanitize history, such as by banning Confederate flags at football games, ordering the school band not to play the song "Dixie," and getting rid of sideline mascot Colonel Reb.

PROGRAM HIGHLIGHTS

NATIONAL CHAMPIONSHIPS (1): 1960

SEC CHAMPIONSHIPS (6): 1947, 1954, 1955, 1960, 1962, 1963

BOWL RECORD: 21-12 (.636). Last bowl—21-7 over Oklahoma State in 2010 Cotton Bowl

LONGEST WINNING STREAK: 13 games, 1955-56

WINNINGEST COACH: John Vaught (1947-70, 1973), 190-61-12 (74.5 percent)

HEISMAN TROPHY WINNERS OR HIGHEST HEISMAN FINISH: Quarterback Archie Manning, 1970 third place; quarterback Eli Manning, 2003 third place

Through changing times, the Ole Miss faithful have tried hard to remember the words of the late Frank E. Everet Jr., an Ole Miss grad from the early 1930s who once wrote:

"There is a valid distinction between The University and Ole Miss even though the separate threads are closely interwoven.

"The University is buildings, trees and people. Ole Miss is mood, emotion and personality. One is physical, and the other is spiritual. One is tangible, and the other intangible.

"The University is respected, but Ole Miss is loved. The University gives a diploma and regretfully terminates tenure, but one never graduates from Ole Miss."

LEGENDS

Johnny Vaught
The only man in SEC history to win the conference championship in his first year as head coach, Vaught won six SEC championships and one national championship from 1947 to 1970 and 1973.

Archie Manning
A running, throwing, scrambling, dynamic, playmaking quarterback from 1968 to 1970, Manning is so beloved that his No. 18 is the official campus speed limit.

Charlie Conerly
"Chunkin'" Charlie started his career at Ole Miss in 1942, left to serve in World War II as a Marine for three years, before returning to Oxford in 1946. As a senior in 1947, he was the SEC's Player of the Year.

Eli Manning
The youngest son of Archie Manning, he obliterated all of his father's records, finishing his four-year career from 2000 to 2003 with 10,119 passing yards and 81 touchdown passes.

NOTABLE ALUMS

James Meredith—First African-American student at Ole Miss and civil rights leader

John Grisham—Ole Miss law school graduate who became best-selling author of legal thrillers

Sharyn Alfonsi—On-air journalist for ABC News

A. C. Wharton Jr.—Current mayor of Memphis

STADIUM

Vaught-Hemingway Stadium: No stadium in the SEC has improved more in a short period of time than Vaught-Hemingway. For almost sixty-five years since it was constructed in 1915 as a 24,000-seat stadium, there had never been an expansion, no modern amenity added. But since 1980, there have been four expansions adding 36,000 seats, including plush club levels and a new press box.

FIGHT SONG

"FORWARD REBELS"

Forward Rebels, march to fame,

Hit that line and win this game,

We know that you'll fight it through,

For your colors Red and Blue—Rah, Rah, Rah.

Rebels you're the Southland's pride,

Take that ball and hit your stride,

Don't stop 'till the victory's won, For your Ole Miss.

Fight, fight for your Ole Miss.

MASCOT

The nickname "Rebels" was chosen in 1936 by an 18-3 vote of newsmen participating in a contest sponsored by Bill Gates (later Ole Miss' sports information director), sports editor of *The Mississippian*, the student newspaper. The original school mascot, Colonel Reb, was created in 1939 but didn't make it to the Ole Miss sideline until 1979. By 2003, the school administration, feeling that Colonel Reb was a reminder of the South's Civil War/plantation days, removed the colonel. In 2011 a vote was taken for a new mascot. After more than 13,000 votes, students, faculty, alumni, staff, and season-ticket holders selected Rebel the Black Bear on April 5, 2011.

MIZZOU CONNECTION

All-time football record vs. Missouri: 1-5

1973: Missouri 17, Mississippi 0 (Columbia)
1974: Mississippi 10, Missouri 0 (Jackson)
1978: Missouri 45, Mississippi 14 (Columbia)
1979: Missouri 33, Mississippi 7 (Jackson)
2006: Missouri 34, Mississippi 7 (Columbia)
2007: Missouri 38, Mississippi 25 (Oxford)

It's been a mostly one-sided series, including a 3-1 run by the Tigers in the 1970s as the Rebels reeled through most of the decade. In 1978, Missouri experienced a sneak preview of what is to come in the SEC with games against Alabama, Ole Miss, and LSU. The series picked back up with a home-and-away contract in 2006-07, and the Rebels were no match for Chase Daniel and MU's high-powered spread attack. Ole Miss had its share of stars during the brief Ed Orgeron regime—including future NFL starters Patrick Willis, Michael Oher, BenJarvus Green-Ellis, and Mike Wallace—but Daniel and the Tigers ran up 471 and 559 yards of offense in the two victories.

The write stuff: Two of America's most influential writers of the twentieth century were students at these respective schools. The great playwright Tennessee Williams came to Columbia in 1929 to study journalism and stayed at Missouri for three years. His entire body of work, which includes the classics *The Glass Menagerie* and *A Streetcar Named Desire*, include twenty-six characters and places inspired by his time at Mizzou. William Faulkner grew up in Oxford, enrolled at Ole Miss in 1920, and spent three semesters on campus before dropping out. He lived in Oxford on and off until his death, and his home is now owned and maintained by the university.

Legacies galore: Ole Miss produced what might be the most famous father-son combo in college football in former quarterbacks Archie and Eli Manning. Missouri hasn't turned out a father-son set of Tigers with that kind of star power, but a few have donned the black and gold. Corby Jones, the Tigers' quarterback from 1995 to 1998, was the son of former MU defensive lineman and assistant coach Curtis Jones. Kirk Farmer quarterbacked the Tigers for parts of three seasons (1999-01), thirty years after his dad, Mike Farmer, played QB and punted for the Tigers. Kevin Potter was an All-Big Eight safety (1979-82), and his son Randy Potter (1995-98) played cornerback and returned kicks. The 2012 Missouri defense includes two second-generation Tigers: linebacker Andrew Wilson, whose father, Jay Wilson (1979-82), was once MU's career tackles leader; and defensive end Shane Ray, whose father, Wendell Ray (1978-80), was a standout defensive end.

GAME DAY

MEDIA

Broadcasting the Game: WQLJ-FM (93.7) in Oxford WHBQ-AM (56) in Memphis

Covering the Rebels: www.clarionledger.com/section/SPORTS030103/UM-Ole-Miss-sports (*The Jackson Clarion-Ledger*), www.commercialappeal.com (*The Commercial Appeal*, Memphis), www.nems360.com/pages/insideolemisssports (*Northeast Mississippi Daily Journal, Tupelo*), www.omspirit.com (*The Ole Miss Spirit*), www.olemiss.rivals.com (RebelGrove)

TAILGATING

A large majority of tailgating at Ole Miss is confined to the Grove, a grassy, shady, ten-acre slice of heaven smack dab in the middle of campus. The Grove is thoroughly policed and anyone publicly drunk will be arrested. Distribution of alcohol without a permit is illegal, and leaving alcohol in plain view or unattended is considered distribution. Unattended tents and coolers are subject to inspection, and alcohol will be confiscated. Ole Miss policy prohibits drinking games and mass or rapid consumption devices such as kegs, funnels, shots). No stakes for tents may be driven in the ground because of electric and water lines. Portable generators with a decibel rating of 60DB or less are permitted. Tailgaters can use electrical outlets on the exterior of campus buildings but can't run extension cords into buildings.

SHUTTLE

Parking close to Vaught-Hemingway is a chore. That's why the City of Oxford has secure parking for just $5 per vehicle at designated sites where there are free round-trip shuttles to the stadium. Sites include the Oxford Middle School, located at 501 Martin Luther King, Jr. Boulevard (corner of Washington Avenue), and the Oxford Activity Center, located at 400 Price Street (corner of Molly Barr Road). Shuttle service starts three hours before kickoff and ends two hours after the game. Drop off is on east side of the stadium at Gates 14, 15, and 16. The shuttle is a great deal, because most public campus parking is $20 per vehicle. The University Police Department (UPD) also provides a shuttle from the Grove to Vaught-Hemingway before, during, and after football games.

TRADITIONS

Hotty Toddy: This is the Rebels' favorite cheer, short and sweet, that picks up steam and is rattled off in speedreading fashion. It starts with a question.

Are you READY?
Hell, YES!
DAMN right!
Hotty Toddy Gosh Almighty,
Who the hell are we? HEY!
Flim Flam, Bim, Bam,
OLE MISS BY DAMN!

Chucky: Chucky Mullins was a cornerback from tiny Russellville, Alabama, who convinced then-Ole Miss coach Billy Brewer to give him a scholarship. Though undersized, Mullins was a vicious hitter who played with extraordinary heart. In the Rebels' Homecoming game against Vanderbilt on October 28, 1989, he was paralyzed tackling Vandy's Brad Gaines. SEC fans raised more than $1 million for Mullins' trust fund. He returned to class in January 1991 but died a few months later because of complications from a blood clot. In the spring of 1990, the Phi Beta Sigma fraternity at Ole Miss initiated the Chucky Mullins Courage Award to be given each spring to a Rebels' defensive player.

B-BALL, ETC.

No Ole Miss team in any sport has won a national championship, but men's tennis under Coach Billy Chadwick has been to the NCAA's Final Four in 1997, 1999, and 2005. With his fifth SEC championship in 2009, Chadwick trails only legendary football coach John Vaught in SEC titles won at Ole Miss.

ABOUT TOWN

Oxford was founded in 1836 when the Chickasaw Indian Cession, a treaty that ordered the removal of most of the Indians in North Mississippi, cleared the way for settlers from Virginia and the Carolinas to find homes there. Immediately, the area was named Lafayette County after Marquis de Lafayette, the French hero of the American Revolution. That same year, three Lafayette residents—John Chisholm, John D. Martin, and John L. Craig—donated fifty acres of centrally located land that had been previously owned by Princess Hoka, a Chickasaw Indian maiden. The land was named Oxford, after the university town of Oxford, England. Twelve years later in 1848, the University of Mississippi opened it doors. In the 1930s, Mississippi Governor Theodore Bilbo tried to relocate the school to Jackson, which would have sounded a death knell for Oxford. But Ole Miss Chancellor Alfred Hume saved the day by giving state legislators such a memorable tour of Ole Miss and Oxford that they voted down Bilbo's legislation.

LODGING

The Inn at Ole Miss: This 146-room, eight-story, all-suite hotel is located on the Ole Miss campus, so everything is in walking distance. The bad news is that this place stays booked in football season. *120 Alumni Dr., University, MS 38677, 888-486-7666, www.theinnatolemiss.com*

Downtown Oxford Inn: There's not a more convenient hotel to enjoy the ambience of downtown Oxford. Ground-level floors and suites step directly out into downtown. *400 North Lamar Blvd., Oxford, MS 38655, 662-234-3031, www.downtownoxfordinn.com*

The 5 Twelve Bed and Breakfast: Located between the downtown square and the Ole Miss campus, this five guest-room house featuring classic Greek Revival architecture couldn't be more quaint. *512 Van Buren Ave., Oxford, MS 662-234-8043, www.the512oxford.com*

EATING

City Grocery: Don't let the name fool you. When's the last time you walked into a grocery with white linen, candlelight, an extensive wine list, and eclectic Southern cuisine featuring such dishes as blue crab fritters and a truffled chicken pot pie? *152 Courthouse Square, Oxford, MS 38655, 662-232-8080, www.citygroceryonline.com*

Ajax Diner: This is absolute comfort food heaven, with eight types of plate lunches with a choice of twenty homemade veggies for sides. Does it get any better than a big hunk of Matty's Mom's meat loaf propped up next to sweet potato casserole and butter beans? *118 Courthouse Square, Oxford, MS 38655, 662-232-8880, www.ajaxdiner.net*

Oby: Well-spiced Cajun food, such as jambalaya and red beans and rice platters, along with a multitude of seafood po-boys (oyster, shrimp, crawfish, catfish, and alligator). Great food at extremely reasonable prices. *1931 University Ave., Oxford, MS 38655, 662-234-4530, www.obys.net*

SIGHTSEEING

Rowan Oak: Originally built in 1844, this was author William Faulkner's home for forty years. It's just south of downtown Oxford Square. The grounds at Rowan Oak are open without charge from dawn to dusk daily, but it's $5 admission to the house.

Center for the Study of Southern Culture: Housed in Barnard Observatory on the Ole Miss campus, the center promotes regional studies. *Grove Loop & Student Union Dr., Oxford, MS 38655, 662-915-5993*

SHOPPING

Square Books: Simply one of the finest, most diverse, and most fascinating book stores in the South where there's always a book signing or book reading happening. *160 Courthouse Square, Oxford, MS 38655, 662-236-2262, www.squarebooks.com*

Neilson's Department Store: Founded in 1839, it's the store generations of Oxford residents have relied on for their fancy duds as well as school clothes. *119 Courthouse Square, Oxford, MS 38655, 800-797-8293, www.neilsons1839.com*

University Sporting Goods: Founded in 1966, a year before a redheaded quarterback from Drew, Mississippi, named Archie Manning showed up on the Ole Miss campus. If you want Ole Miss souvenirs—even Ole Miss band-aids—this is the place to find it. *105 Courthouse Square, Oxford, MS 38655, 662-234-1736, www.rebelfever.com*

NIGHTLIFE

Proud Larry's: Undisputed best live music venue in Oxford that also serves some mighty tasty hand-tossed pizzas like the Fat Larry. *211 South Lamar, Oxford, MS 38655, 662-236-0050, www.proudlarrys.com*

The Library Bar and Grill: Bar food, bands, flat screens, and plenty of room make this one of downtown Oxford's best multi-purpose venues. *120 South 11th St., Oxford, MS 38655, 662-234-1411*

The Lyric, Oxford: Located in a building constructed in the 1800s and converted into a theatre in the 1920s, the Lyric is a concert venue attracting a variety of eclectic acts. *1006 Van Buren Ave., Oxford, MS 38655, 662-234-5333, www.thelyricoxford.com*

TRAVELING TO OXFORD?

It's one of the few drivable trips in the SEC for Missourians, especially from the east side of the state where it's a straight shot down I-55, about 360 miles from St. Louis. From the west side of Missouri, cutting south through Springfield is the shorter path, but it's still five hundred-plus miles from Kansas City. If you'd rather fly, Memphis International Airport is the most convenient spot, just a seventy-mile drive from Ole Miss. The Mizzou Alumni Association hosts a Tiger Tailgate. Visit MizzouSportsTravel.com for more information on tickets and pricing.

SOUTH CAROLINA

The University of South Carolina started with a single building in 1805. South Carolina College, as it was called in those days, is a school that made it through the Civil War and Reconstruction, closings, and name changes.

Because of a lack of students, the school closed in 1861 at the onset of the Civil War. But it re-opened in 1866 as the University of South Carolina. South Carolina was the only state university in the South to admit and grant degrees to African-American students during Reconstruction, starting in 1873.

Following the end of Reconstruction in 1877, the state's conservative leaders closed the university again and then reopened it in 1880 as an all-white agricultural college. In 1892, the agricultural school fielded its first football team, with no coach and no captain, and lost its only game, 44-0, to Furman.

UNIVERSITY OF SOUTH CAROLINA

Students: 29,957

Columbia: pop. 129,272

Williams-Brice Stadium: seats 80,250

Colors: Garnet and Black

Nickname: Gamecocks

Mascot: Cocky

Campus Attractions: The Horseshoe, location of the school's first building; the Cockaboose Railroad

Phone: 803-777-7000 (general information)
803-777-8400 (campus police)
803-777-4202 (athletic department)

Tickets: 803-777-4274

In 1906, the institution was re-chartered for the final time as the University of South Carolina, but African-American students wouldn't be admitted again until the 1960s. The school posted five straight winning football seasons from 1902 to 1907 (no team in 1906) and wouldn't string together that many consecutive winning seasons until seven straight from 1928 to 1934.

South Carolina, as a member of the old Southern Conference, went to its first bowl game on January 1, 1946, and lost to Wake Forest, 26-14, in the inaugural Gator Bowl. The Gamecocks didn't play in another bowl for twenty-three years until the 1969 Peach Bowl and lost again, 14-3, to West Virginia. However, Coach Paul Dietzel led the Gamecocks to a perfect 6-0 record in the Atlantic Coast Conference and was named the league's coach of the year that season.

Overall, South Carolina lost its first eight bowl games. Even with Heisman Trophy winner George Rogers, the Gamecocks fell to Missouri in the 1979 Hall of Fame Bowl and the following year to Pittsburgh in their second Gator Bowl appearance. Over a two-year period in 1979-80, the Gamecocks posted back-to-back 8-4 records.

The next plateau came under Coach Joe Morrison in 1984 when the Gamecocks reeled off nine straight victories before losing to Navy. The ten victories that season were the most in school history until the 2011 team posted eleven wins. After a close victory over Clemson, South Carolina lost to Oklahoma State in the Gator Bowl but still finished as the No. 11 team in the final Associated Press Poll in 1984.

The Gamecocks joined the SEC for the 1992 season, but they didn't enjoy much success until Lou Holtz became the head coach and finally posted the school's

PROGRAM HIGHLIGHTS

NATIONAL CHAMPIONSHIPS (0): South Carolina has had mixed results in football over the years while it competed under the banners of the Southern and Atlantic Coast Conferences and later as an independent before joining the Southeastern Conference.

ACC CHAMPIONSHIPS (1): 1969 South Carolina was a charter member of the Atlantic Coast Conference but withdrew in 1971 and became an independent.

SEC CHAMPIONSHIPS (0): South Carolina only joined the conference for the 1992 season. The Gamecocks won the 2010 Eastern Division championship before falling to eventual national champion Auburn in the SEC title game.

BOWL RECORD: 5-12 (.416). Last bowl—30-13 victory over Nebraska in the 2012 Capital One Bowl

LONGEST WINNING STREAK: 9 games, 1984

WINNINGEST COACH: Steve Spurrier (2005-), 55-35, 63.6 percent (by percentage, with more than two seasons as head coach)

HEISMAN TROPHY WINNERS OR HIGHEST HEISMAN FINISH: Running back George Rogers, 1980 winner

first winning SEC mark in 2000 (5-3). Steve Spurrier took the Gamecocks a step further in 2010 with the school's first SEC East title.

LEGENDS

George Rogers

As the school's only Heisman Trophy winner, Rogers has a special place in the hearts of Gamecock fans. He led the country in rushing in 1980 and was the first player chosen in the 1981 NFL Draft by the New Orleans Saints. He later played for the 1988 Super Bowl Champion Washington Redskins.

Sterling Sharpe

Sharpe finished his career as the Gamecocks' all-time leading receiver (at the time) with nearly 2,500 yards. He was a first-round draft pick by the Green Bay Packers in 1988. Sharpe's jersey was retired following the 1987 regular season. During his career at South Carolina (1983, 1985-87), he caught at least one pass in thirty-four straight games.

Lou Holtz

Holtz jump-started South Carolina's program and handed off to Steve Spurrier before the 2005 season. The current ESPN analyst registered back-to-back victories in the Outback Bowl and top twenty finishes in 2000 and 2001, both firsts in school history.

Steve Wadiak

Wadiak led South Carolina in rushing and scoring in all four seasons he played from 1948 to 1951. After rushing for 2,878 yards, he stood as the Gamecocks' leading rusher for twenty-nine years, until Rogers passed him in 1980. Wadiak's No. 37 became the first retired by the school in 1951 after he was killed in an automobile accident.

STADIUM

Williams-Brice: The stadium opened in 1934 and was constructed by the Works Progress Administration. Seating just 17,600 fans at that point, the stadium has undergone several expansions to move past 80,000 in capacity, with many improvements and some additions coming in the last decade. The stadium was dedicated as Williams-Brice Stadium in 1972 after a wealthy Gamecocks benefactor Mrs. Martha Williams-Brice, whose husband Thomas H. Brice was a football letterman from 1922 to 1924. Nephews of Mrs. Brice passed on a substantial inheritance to the university, including a bequest for the stadium funding.

NOTABLE ALUMS

W.W. "Hootie" Johnson—Former chairman of the executive committee of Bank of America and chairman emeritus of the Augusta National Golf Club

Hootie and the Blowfish (Dean Felber, Mark Bryan, Jim Sonefield, Darius Rucker)—Grammy Award—winning musicians

Charlie Weis—Former head football coach at Notre Dame and now at Kansas, he is a four-time assistant coach of Super Bowl championship teams

Gary Parsons—Founder of XM Satellite Radio and former executive vice president of MCI

MASCOT

Cocky became the school's mascot in 1980, replacing Big Spur. During the last thirty years Cocky has become a staple in Columbia. Cocky revs up the fans during a 2001 Magic Box entrance when the Gamecock football team enters the home stadium for games.

Cocky is symbolic of the Fighting Gamecocks, the nickname adopted at the turn of the twentieth century for the school because observers likened the feisty squads to gamecocks—fighting roosters known to participate in fights to the death. Very popular in the nineteenth century, cock fighting has been outlawed by most states for humanitarian reasons.

Originally, the "Fighting Gamecock" referred to Thomas Sumter, a fierce and courageous fighter from South Carolina in the American Revolution. A British general said the brigadier general of the South Carolina Militia "fought like a gamecock."

FIGHT SONG

"THE FIGHTING GAMECOCKS LEAD THE WAY"

Hey, let's give a cheer, Carolina is here,

The Fighting Gamecocks lead the way.

Who gives a care if the going gets tough,

And when it is rough, that's when the 'Cocks get going.

Hail to our colors of Garnet and Black,

In Carolina pride have we.

So, Go Gamecocks Go—FIGHT!

Drive for the goal—FIGHT!

USC will win today—GO COCKS!

So, let's give a cheer, Carolina is here.

The Fighting Gamecocks All the Way!

MIZZOU CONNECTION

All-time football record vs. Missouri: 0-2

1979: Missouri 24, South Carolina 14
(Hall of Fame Bowl, Birmingham, Ala.)

2005: Missouri 38, South Carolina 31
(Independence Bowl, Shreveport, La.)

Courtesy Mizzou Athletics Media Relations

After finishing the 1979 regular season 6-5, Missouri players initially threatened to boycott the Hall of Fame Bowl against South Carolina. But Mizzou's potent running game outshined the Gamecock attack led by future Heisman Trophy winner George Rogers. His 133 yards weren't enough as MVP quarterback Phil Bradley guided an offense that controlled the line of scrimmage and outgained the Gamecocks 289-263. The more memorable matchup came in 2005 when the Tigers needed the greatest comeback in team history after falling behind 21-0 just eight minutes into the game. Marcus King's 99-yard interception return sparked the rally, and in his final college game, quarterback Brad Smith punctuated the win with 432 yards of offense and three rushing touchdowns.

Two of a kind: The hometowns for both campuses share the most fundamental feature: a name. Columbia, S.C., was created by the state's general assembly in 1786, and in an 11-7 vote by the state senate, Columbia was chosen as the town's name over Washington. With a nod to explorer Christopher Columbus, the word *Columbia* was considered a colonial alternative for America. In 1821, a small group of settlers in Missouri chose the same name for their new home after moving from the nearby village of Smithton. Both towns are also home to Columbia College. The South Carolina school is a private women's college founded in 1854. The Missouri version, also originally a private women's college, was founded three years earlier and became co-ed in 1970.

Homegrown: Both Columbia, Missouri, and Columbia, S.C., lay claim to producing a tasty barbeque sauce. Kansas City might be Missouri's most famous home for barbeque, but for nearly forty years, some of the state's finest has been brewed in the Columbia basement of Harry and Lina Berrier. Since 1975, local grocers have sold their popular tomato-based concoction, Show-Me Liquid Smoke Bar-B-Q Sauce. In Columbia, S.C., the sauce is yellow because of its mustard base, the preferred flavor of the region. The most famous place to chow is Maurice's BBQ Piggie Park, run by Maurice Bessinger, whose barbeque is smothered in his Southern Gold family recipe.

GAME DAY

MEDIA

Broadcasting the Game: WNKT-FM (107.5) and WISW-AM (1320) in Columbia. All Gamecock football broadcasts also can be heard on Sirius XM.

Covering the Gamecocks: www.thestate.com/sports (*The State*), www.postandcourier.com/news/sports (*Charleston Post & Courier*)

TAILGATING

RV parking is available in the Fairgrounds (803-799-3387) on the east side of Assembly Street and at Gate 12 on Rosewood Drive. Also, RV parking is available at Capital City Stadium/Blowfish Park, which is located less than a half-mile from the stadium to the west side of Assembly Street. Parking in this lot costs $10 per space needed to fully accommodate the vehicle. RV hook-ups are not available in this lot. On the Friday before the SEC home games, this lot will open at 2:00 p.m. for overnight RV parking. The same parking fees are in effect. Additional RV parking is available on Fridays of SEC games and game day at the Farmers' Market. Parking is limited and based on first-come, first-serve. Entrance is on National Guard Road, which is off Bluff Road at the practice field. Game-day RV parking is $60 and also $60 for Friday parking. This lot opens at 2:00 p.m. on Fridays. The Farmers' Market is at 1001 Bluff Rd., Columbia, SC 29201.

For tailgating, tents should be no larger than 10′ x 10′ and should be contained within the individual parking space. Tents should be dismantled prior to guests leaving for the game. Unattended tents are subject to removal by university officials at their discretion. Drive areas must be cleared enough to allow access for emergency vehicles. Gas grilling is permitted. Charcoal grilling is prohibited for safety reasons.

Gamecock Village is located across from the stadium in the Biscuit House parking lot. It opens four hours prior to kickoff and includes interactive games, sponsor displays, and appearances by the USC cheerleaders and band.

SHUTTLE

Shuttle service is available for $3 per person round trip. Service begins three hours prior to kickoff and runs until one and a half hours after the game with limited service throughout the game. Pickups are Colonial Life Arena/Coliseum Lot B and Blowfish Stadium. Drop-off is on Rosewood, east of Main Gate to Fairgrounds. Post-game pickup is on Rosewood, east of Main Gate to Fairgrounds. Post-game drop-offs are at Colonial Life Arena/Coliseum Lot B and Blowfish Stadium.

TRADITIONS

Cockaboose Train: South Carolina fans have flocked to a game-day tailgating tradition that was first started here: twenty-two immobile cabooses line a railroad track outside Williams-Brice Stadium. Each is a private tailgating area where owners of the cabooses have decorated, in some cases extravagantly. The interiors of cabooses are treated like condos, with an association. Other events can be held in the cabooses that are sometimes rented out by the owners. Game days are the big events.

"2001" Opening of Game: The theme song of *2001—A Space Oydssey* is the background music for the pre-game entrance of the Gamecock football team. Corresponding to the University of South Carolina's Bicentennial in 2001, the theme song stokes the partisan home crowd into a fever pitch.

B-BALL, ETC.

Gamecock men's basketball has had some success in recent years, winning back-to-back National Invitation Tournament titles in 2005 and 2006. But recent NCAA Tournament success has been limited. The heyday for Gamecock basketball was under Frank McGuire from 1967 to 1976 when the team went to three NCAA Tournament Sweet Sixteens. Now, let's talk about baseball. That's the sport, other than football, that makes the headlines in Columbia. The Gamecocks became only the sixth school in NCAA history to win back-to-back NCAA titles in 2010 and 2011. Since 1975, the Gamecocks have made ten appearances in the College World Series.

ABOUT TOWN

Columbia is the state capital of South Carolina (since 1786) and the largest city in the state. It was selected as the capital because of its central location in the state. In recent years, Columbia has undergone a revitalization in several areas in the city's core. It is considered one of the best places in the country to retire and is home to several other smaller colleges and universities.

LODGING

Plan Ahead. Hotels fill up quickly. You can go to www.columbiacvb.com for a list of hotels in Columbia and surrounding areas. But here are a few of the highlight hotels of the non-chain variety:

The Whitney Hotel: An all-suite property located in the historic Shandon neighborhood is minutes away from a variety of specialty shops and restaurants. *700 Woodrow St., Columbia, SC 29205, 803-252-0845, www. whitneyhotel.com*

Inn at USC: This elegant boutique hotel, located on the historic campus of the University of South Carolina in the heart of downtown Columbia, boasts 117 luxurious guest rooms. Originally, this hotel was the Black House, a home built in 1910. *1619 Pendleton St., Columbia, SC 29201, 803-779-7779, www.innatusc. com*

The Inn at Claussen's: This is a stylish twenty-eight-room boutique hotel located in the heart of Columbia's charming Five Points, within walking distance of the University of South Carolina. Once known as Claussen's Bakery, the converted inn is listed on the National Register of Historic Places. *2003 Greene St., Columbia, SC 29205, 803-765-0440, www.theinnatclaussens.com*

EATING

Yesterday's: A Columbia staple for more than thirty-five years. There's an on-site prep kitchen. Each day begins with a selection of farmers' market vegetables, and the freshest chicken, beef, and seafood are added. The menu "offers a wide variety of international dishes and Southern favorites." Daily specials change by the season. *2030 Devine St., Five Points, Columbia, SC 29205, 803-799-0196, www.yesterdayssc.com*

Liberty Tap Room: One of four locations in the state, Liberty offers a variety of brews on tap, including some of the bar's own, such as Rocket's Red Ale. Check out the menu and Sunday brunch. Varied daily menu with steaks, seafood, and "comfort food." *828 Gervais St., Columbia, SC 29201, 803-461-4677, www. libertytaproom.com*

Maurice's Bar-B-Q: They had to quit flying the Confederate Battle Flag atop the Columbia location because of dry-cleaning costs . . . hmm. Maybe it will pop back up by the time you arrive. The barbeque is lip-smacking good. Sweet tea, pulled pork sandwiches, great sauce. *1600 Charleston Hwy., West Columbia, SC 29169, 803-796-0220, www.piggiepark.com*

SIGHTSEEING

McKissick Museum: Located on the historic Horseshoe of the University South Carolina Campus, it features folk life displays and exhibits. Open to the public and free of charge. Closed on Sundays and on all university and state holidays. Hours 8:30 a.m.-5 p.m. (Mon.-Fri.); 11 a.m.-3 p.m. (Sat.).

Riverbanks Zoo and Garden: (Main Entrance) 500 Wildlife Parkway, just off I-126 at Greystone Boulevard. Admission: $11.75 (Adults); $9.25 (Children 3-12); Free (2 and under). Good for a day trip or just an afternoon with the kids before the big game. Hours 9 a.m.-5 p.m., extended an hour from April 2 to early October.

River Alliance's Three Rivers Greenway: Eight and a half miles of pathway along the area's rivers bordering the cities of Columbia, West Columbia, and Cayce. The lighted and paved trails are equipped with emergency call boxes, clean bathroom areas, and water fountains. Fans can stroll, jog, bike, or blade. Casual walkers, hand-in-hand or hand-to-leash, can stop to read informational wayside exhibits on the history and habitat of the area, or can picnic at a scenic spot overlooking the water. All areas of the Greenway are dog friendly, and all paths are ADA accessible, accommodating baby strollers and wheelchairs.

SHOPPING

Congaree Vista: Once a bustling cotton warehouse district and commercial railroad terminal, the Vista area of downtown Columbia had declined severely by the late 1970s. But now it is back to life, with dozens of specialty stores along with restaurants and bars. *www.vistacolumbia.com/thevistaguild.aspx*

Cotton Mill Exchange: This 3,000-square-foot store is part of the South Carolina State Museum in Columbia open 10 a.m.-5 p.m. Tuesday through Saturday and 1-5 p.m. on Sunday. The store offers a vast selection of merchandise reflecting the culture and heritage of South Carolina. *301 Gervais St., Columbia, SC 29201, 803-898-4967, www.scmuseum.org/store*

NIGHTLIFE

Art Bar: The place to be in Columbia, late-night. A great dance experience underground in an eclectic and artistic atmosphere. Live music. *Located in the Vista area at 1211 Park St., Columbia, SC 29201, 803-929-0198, www.artbarsc.com*

Delaney's Music Pub and Eatery: Irish pub where there is live music five nights a week. Caters to all ages. There are twenty-six beers on tap. Pint nights on Wednesday nights. Trivia on Sundays. *741 Saluda Ave., Columbia, SC 29205, 803-799-3705*

TRAVELING TO COLUMBIA, SOUTH CAROLINA?

It's almost nine hundred miles from Columbia to Columbia, so Tiger fans can forget about driving. Instead, you can book a flight into Columbia Metropolitan Airport with a stop in Atlanta or fly into Charlotte Douglass International and drive the ninety-five miles to Columbia. The Mizzou Alumni Association hosts a Tiger Tailgate. Visit MizzouSportsTravel.com for more information on tickets and pricing.

TENNESSEE

The University of Tennessee endured eighty-five years, two closures, one war, and four name changes to become the school it is today. The journey has been long and hard, first with much doubt and then replaced with determination. But the effort has given the school its indomitable spirit that lives on today.

The school opened in 1794 as Blount College in what is now downtown Knoxville, two years before Tennessee was granted statehood. Cost of tuition was the same as a decent meal at Taco Bell today, about eight dollars. When Blount struggled for funding, it was closed for a decade before reopening as East Tennessee College in 1820. It was re-named again (East Tennessee University) in 1840, closed again for the Civil War, and opened yet again in 1866 after the war-ravaged campus was rebuilt.

Three years later—the Tennessee state legislature designated the school as the state's federal land-grant institution—the school finally benefited from the Morrill Act of 1862, which granted federal land to a university with the stipulation that the school uses the land for education. The school was able to purchase three hundred acres of land for $30,000. Finally in 1879, the state legislature changed the school's name to the University of Tennessee.

UNIVERSITY OF TENNESSEE

Students: 28,000

Knoxville: pop. 178,874

Neyland Stadium: seats 104,079

Colors: Orange and White

Nickname: Volunteers

Mascot: Smokey

Campus Attractions: The Rock, UT Football Hall of Fame exhibit

Phone: 865-974-1000 (general information)
865-974-3114 (campus police)
865-974-1220 (men's athletic department)
865-974-4275 (women's athletic department)

Tickets: 865-656-1200 or 800-332-VOLS (8657)
UTTIX.com

By that time, the school had started a semblance of an athletic program. Tennessee played its first football game in 1891 and in 1921 opened its home stadium—Shields-Watkins Field—named after William S. Shields and his wife Alice Watkins Shields, the financial backers of the field.

In 1925, four years after UT's new football home opened, Robert R. Neyland, an army captain, was hired by the school as an ROTC instructor and the Vols' backfield coach. He was promoted to head coach in 1926 when Coach M. B. Banks became ill and resigned to coach at Knoxville's Central High School.

Because of his army obligations, Neyland's twenty-one seasons as UT's head coach were split into three stints—nine years (1926-34) when his rank was captain, five seasons (1936-40) when he was a major, and seven seasons as a general (1946-52). His 1938, 1939, and 1940 teams won SEC titles and thirty-one of thirty-three games, outscoring opponents by a combined 837 to 75. His 1938 team recorded ten straight shutout wins before losing 14-0 in Southern Cal in the Rose Bowl.

He won 173 games, five SEC titles, and five national championships, but his last in 1951 is the only one officially recognized by the SEC because it included the AP and UPI.

Neyland created seven maxims—things that he felt won games—and his team recited them before every game. The maxims have remained the foundation of UT football philosophy and are still recited before games today.

The maxims are:

- The team that makes the fewest mistakes will win.
- Play for and make the breaks and when one comes your way—SCORE.
- If at first the game—or the breaks—go against you, don't let up . . . put on more steam.
- Protect our kickers, our QB, our lead, and our ball game.
- Ball, oskie, cover, block, cut and slice, pursue, and gang tackle . . . for

PROGRAM HIGHLIGHTS

NATIONAL CHAMPIONSHIPS (2): 1951, 2010

SEC CHAMPIONSHIPS (13): 1938, 1939 (tied), 1940, 1946 (tied), 1951 (tied), 1956, 1967, 1969, 1985, 1989 (tied), 1990, 1997, 1998

BOWL RECORD: 25-24 (.510). Last bowl—30-27 loss in two overtimes to North Carolina in 2010 Music City Bowl

LONGEST WINNING STREAK: 23 games, 1937-39

WINNINGEST COACH: Gen. Robert R. Neyland (1926-34, 1936-40, 1946-52), 173-31-12, 82.9 percent

HEISMAN TROPHY WINNERS OR HIGHEST HEISMAN FINISH: Tailback Hank Lauricella, 1951 runner-up; tailback Johnny Majors, 1956 runner-up; quarterback Heath Shuler, 1993 runner-up; quarterback Peyton Manning, 1996 runner-up

this is the WINNING EDGE.
- Press the kicking game. Here is where the breaks are made.
- Carry the fight to our opponent and keep it there for sixty minutes.

Though Tennessee has had a long line of great players and good coaches after Neyland retired in 1952 to become UT's athletic director, it took the Vols forty-seven years and seven head coaches to win another national title. That happened in 1998 when a Phillip Fulmer–coached Tennessee closed a 13-0 season by beating Florida State in the first BCS championship game.

Since then, Tennessee has gone thirteen seasons without winning an SEC championship, the second longest league title drought in UT history.

LEGENDS

Gen. Robert R. Neyland

Neyland coached five SEC championship teams and four teams that won some form of a national championship (the last in 1951 recognized by the AP and UPI).

Peyton Manning

Strong-armed quarterback blessed with a computer-chip mind and quarterback genes as the son of former Ole Miss and NFL star Archie Manning. Peyton was third on the SEC career list in passing yards (11,201) and second in TD passes (89).

Johnny Majors

The oldest of four football-playing brothers, Majors was a triple-threat single-wing tailback who finished second in the 1956 Heisman Trophy voting. He returned to UT in 1977 as head coach and won 115 games and three SEC titles in sixteen seasons.

Condredge Holloway

First African-American starting quarterback in SEC history, he turned down football offers from his home-state schools Alabama and Auburn because they wanted him to play defensive back, not QB.

NOTABLE ALUMS

James Denton—Actor in TV series *Desperate Housewives*

Deana Carter—Country music singer

Dave Ramsey—Financial author and syndicated radio host

Jim Haslam—Founder of Pilot Corporation, the largest chain of travel centers and truck stops in the United States

---

FIGHT SONG

"ROCKY TOP"

Wish that I was on ole Rocky Top,

Down in the Tennessee hills.

Ain't no smoggy smoke on Rocky Top,

Ain't no telephone bills.

Once there was a girl on Rocky Top,

Half bear the other half cat.

Wild as a mink, sweet as soda pop, I still dream about that.

(Chorus)

Rocky Top, you'll always be

Home sweet home to me.

Good ole Rocky Top,

Rocky Top Tennessee, Rocky Top Tennessee.

Once two strangers climbed on Rocky Top,

Lookin' for a moonshine still.

Strangers ain't come back from Rocky Top,

Guess they never will.

Corn won't grow at all on Rocky Top,

Dirt's too rocky by far.

That's why all the folks on Rocky Top

Get their corn from a jar.

(Chorus)

Now I've had years of cramped up city life,

Trapped like a duck in a pen.

Now all I know is it's a pity life.

Can't be simple again.

(Chorus)

STADIUM

Neyland Stadium: Neyland Stadium is one of college football's grandest arenas, built in 1921 and expanded and renovated seventeen times, with a playing surface that has gone from grass to artificial turf back to grass. It is the third largest stadium in college football with 102,455 seats, and somehow the Vols packed in 109,061 for its 2004 game against Florida in what is believed to be the biggest crowd in SEC history for a regular-season game.

MASCOTS

Smokey: Blue tick hounds named Smokey have been on the Tennessee sideline since 1953. At halftime of the Mississippi State game that season, in a contest to select a coonhound as UT's live mascot, each hound was introduced and the judging was done by student body applause. When the last hound was introduced, named Blue Smokey, the dog barked. The students cheered more, and Smokey tossed back his head and barked again. He kept barking, the crowd went crazy, and Tennessee had found its mascot. Today, Smokey IV has been on duty for the Vols since 2004.

MIZZOU CONNECTION

Courtesy Mizzou Athletics Media Relations

All-time football record vs. Missouri: 0-0

Heading into the 2012 season, Tennessee and Missouri have collectively played 2,397 college football games— but never against each other. In its 116 years of college football, Tennessee has played at least one game against all but ten teams in the six major BCS conferences: Connecticut, South Florida, West Virginia, Illinois, Michigan State, Arizona, Arizona State, Stanford, Washington . . . and Missouri. The Tigers have played three teams from the state of Tennessee—a combined eight games against Memphis, Middle Tennessee, and Vanderbilt—but never the Volunteers.

Country first: Not even the U.S. military could keep these schools' legendary coaches away from campus forever. After the 1934 season, Tennessee coach Robert Neyland sat out one year when the army called him into active service in Panama. W. H. Britton coached the Vols to a 4-5 record in 1935, but Neyland was back on the sideline in 1936 and coached another five seasons in Knoxville . . . until he was again recalled by the military. He returned to UT for a third stint from 1946 to 1952 and later served as the school's athletic director. Missouri's Don Faurot did much the same, coaching the Tigers from 1935 to 1942 before serving three years in the Navy during World War II. He returned to MU in 1946 and coached another eleven seasons. Like Neyland, Faurot served many years as athletic director. Both coaches are also the namesake of their respective team's home facilities: Neyland Stadium and Faurot Field.

Rookie rituals: Both schools have established traditions to officially welcome incoming freshmen to campus. At Tennessee, the freshmen participate in Torch Night, a candlelight ceremony where the newcomers pledge a loyalty oath to the university and are formally declared part of the student body. At Missouri, freshmen assemble on the Francis Quadrangle the eve before classes begin and walk through the campus's famous Columns and toward Jesse Hall, symbolizing their entrance into the university. At the end of their walk, students are greeted by faculty and staff offering cups of Tiger Stripe ice cream, a blend of French vanilla and dark Dutch chocolate created on campus at Buck's Ice Cream Parlor.

GAME DAY

MEDIA

Broadcasting the Game: WIVK-FM 107.7 (Knoxville), WNRQ-FM 105.9 Nashville, WMFS-FM (92.9) Memphis

Covering the Vols: www.govolsxtra.com (*Knoxville News Sentinel*), www.tennessean.com/section/SPORTS0601/Sports-Tennessee-Volunteers (*The Tennessean*, Nashville), www.timesfreepress.com/news/sports/ (*Chattanooga Times Free Press*)

TAILGATING

Tailgates aren't allowed before 7 a.m. on game day and must be packed by midnight unless it's a night kickoff. No open fires or tents are allowed. Adhere to Knoxville's strict open-container policy. It's best if you keep your mixed drink in a cup and your liquor out of sight.

SHUTTLE

Starting three hours before kickoff, numerous city buses transport fans to Neyland Stadium from the Civic Coliseum, Old City, and Market Square area of downtown at a round-trip cost of $5 per person. Also, starting three hours before kickoff, eight buses run from Farragut High School off Campbell Station Road to Neyland at a round-trip cost of $15 per person. A free shuttle is available from the Ag Campus.

TRADITIONS

Checkerboard End Zones: The idea for the Vols' checkerboard end zones came from former Tennessee football coach and athletic director Doug Dickey. When Dickey took over as coach in 1964, he had the end zones painted with the checkerboards. Each end zone contains 125' x 5' squares. It costs $800 of paint per home game—twenty gallons at forty dollars per gallon—to paint the checkerboards.

Vol Navy: What started as a quicker way to get to Neyland Stadium for former Vols broadcaster George Mooney in 1962 has turned into a unique tradition. Rather that fight game-day traffic, Mooney navigated his small boat down the Tennessee River and docked next to the stadium. Now, about two hundred boats begin arriving days in advance of a home game, forming one heck of floating tailgate party.

B-BALL, ETC.

No college in America has impacted the sport of women's basketball like Tennessee. The Lady Vols have won eight national championships under the leadership of retired coach Pat Summitt, the all-time winningest coach in college history. Summitt, who stepped down in the spring of 2012, also had a 100 percent graduation rate for players who finish their careers. Tennessee's men's and women's track programs have won a combined six national championships, ten Olympic medals, and have had at least one track athlete in every Summer Olympics dating back to 1964.

ABOUT TOWN

Knoxville was originally hunting grounds for the Cherokee Indians before James White, the city's founder, established his home in 1786 as a fort and cluster of cabins. The town was renamed Knoxville in 1791 and became one of the South's leading distribution centers. Knoxville's downtown area declined after the 1920s. After the city hosted the 1982 World's Fair, which drew eleven million visitors, downtown made a comeback that is still going strong today.

LODGING

Four Points by Sheraton Cumberland House Hotel: Knoxville has the number one Four Points by Sheraton hotel in North America for overall guest satisfaction for three straight years and former Starwood "Hotel of the Year." It's one mile from the UT campus. *1109 White Ave., Knoxville, TN 37916, 865-971-4663, www.starwoodhotels.com*

The Oliver Hotel: Built in 1876 as a bakery in downtown Knoxville, the Oliver morphed into a hotel in 1982. A 2011 renovation changed this same ol' same ol' hotel into a charming boutique hotel that has earned rave reviews for its eclectic style, sophistication, and service. *407 Union Ave., Knoxville, TN 37902, 865-521-0050, www.theoliverhotel.com*

Hilton Knoxville Airport: If you're flying into Knoxville, this hotel is a one hundred-yard walk under a covered walkway from baggage claim at McGhee-Tyson Airport. Convenient? You're practically sleeping in the control tower and just fifteen minutes from Neyland Stadium. *2001 Alcoa Highway, Alcoa, TN 37701, 865-970-4300*

EATING

Ye Olde Steak House: This steak house boasts twenty-ounce cuts of meat, unbelievable side dishes like woodshed potatoes (peppery fried potato rounds with smothered onions), salads with homemade dressing, and a fifteen-deep menu of homemade desserts like the red velvet cake (chocolate cake with layers of cream cheese frosting). *6838 Chapman Hwy., Knoxville, TN 37920, 865-577-9328, www.yeoldesteakhouse.com*

Calhoun's on the River: Go for the Calhoun's Trio (baby back ribs, chicken tenders, hickory smoked pork) and a slice of key lime pie, then call 911 for a ride back to your hotel. *400 Neyland Dr., Knoxville, TN 37902, 865-673-3355, www.coppercellar.com/Restaurant-Calhouns.html*

Litton's Market and Restaurant: There's nothing better than a hamburger with fresh ground meat on buns that have just been baked, or a thick steak surrounded by homegrown vegetables. You get both here. *2803 Essary Rd., Knoxville, TN 37918, 865-688-0429, www.littonsburgers.com*

SIGHTSEEING

Knoxville Zoo: There are more than eight hundred animals, with everything from elephants to penguins to rattlesnakes. Admission is $19.95 for adults, $15.95 for children ages 2 to 12 years old. *350 Knoxville Zoo Dr., Knoxville, TN 37914, 865-637-5331, www.knoxville-zoo.org*

The Women's Basketball Hall of Fame: Where could you have this amazing 32,000-square-foot shrine to women's hoops but in the backyard of the eight-time NCAA national champion Lady Vols? It's filled with multimedia presentations and memorabilia. Admission is $7.95 adults, $5.95 for children ages 6 to 15. *700 Hall of Fame Dr., Knoxville, TN 37915, 865-633-9000, www.wbhof.com*

SHOPPING

Turkey Creek: Just off Interstate 40 in West Knoxville, this development has more than one hundred shops and restaurants, featuring almost every national brand you know and love. *www.turkeycreekknoxville.com*

Sevierville, Gatlinburg, and Pigeon Forge outlet malls: Scoot twenty-five or so miles southeast of Knoxville on Highway 441 and you will reach the mecca of outlet malls in the bustling Smoky Mountain tourist hamlets of Seiverville, Gatlinburg, and Pigeon Forge.

NIGHTLIFE

Cotton Eyed Joe: The country bar/concert venue has it all—national acts, great drink and food specials every night, and a verrry attractive clientele. Mercy, are those jeans spray-painted on you? *11220 Outlet Dr., Knoxville, TN 37932, 423-675-3563, www.cottoneyedjoe.com*

New Amsterdam Bar and Grill: Two-level bar in the heart of "The Strip" bordering the UT campus, this is Knoxville's premier dance club. Huge dance floor, awesome sound and light systems. Friday night is Ladies Night, featuring 1980s and 1990s music. *1836 Cumberland Ave., Knoxville, TN 37914, 865-934-9606, www.newamsterdamknoxville.com*

SoccerTaco: A Mexican sports bar in Rocky Top country? How does this work? Muy bien, senor. A key lime margarita, a grand slam burrito filled with beer-simmered chicken from scratch, Mexican delights, and more than ten flat-screens tuned into sporting events around the world. You might set up a cot here and never leave. *9 Market Sq., Ste. 101, Knoxville, TN 37902, 865-544-4471, www.soccertaco.com*

TRAVELING TO KNOXVILLE?

You can drive south through Nashville or east through Louisville, but either way it's just over six hundred miles from Columbia to UT's campus. Knoxville's McGhee Tyson Airport offers nonstop flights to Memphis, but from St. Louis, Kansas City, or Springfield you would need a connection flight. Otherwise, airports in Asheville, N.C.; Chattanooga, Tennessee; Lexington, Kentucky; and Nashville are all within about 150 miles. The Mizzou Alumni Association hosts a Tiger Tailgate. Visit MizzouSportsTravel.com for more information on tickets and pricing.

TEXAS A&M

The Morrill Land-Grant College Act is to thank for the oldest public institution of higher education in the state of Texas. Yes, A&M is older than that school to the west decked in burnt orange.

According to the federal legislation, the Morrill Act granted public land to the states for the purpose of financing schools of higher education, "where the leading object shall be, without excluding other scientific and classical studies, and including military tactics, to teach such branches of learning as are related to agriculture and mechanic arts." In 1876, near the banks of the Brazos River, the Agricultural and Mechanical College of Texas was born.

The state university, located in the East Texas town of Bryan and known as Texas AMC, went years before solidifying its own identity. Only males were allowed to enroll, and all students were required to participate in the Corps of Cadets. But the school focused its courses on classical studies, languages, literature, and applied mathematics rather than agricultural studies, sparking protests over the curriculum from locals. The administration was ousted in 1879, but enrollment began to suffer, and Texas AMC's future was in jeopardy as the new University of Texas began to grow in power and prestige.

But in 1891, Lawrence Sullivan Ross, the former governor of Texas and a Texas Ranger, took over as president and rewrote the playbook. Ross rescued the

TEXAS A&M UNIVERSITY

Students: 49,861

Bryan/College Station: pop. 170,058

Kyle Field: seats 83,002

Colors: Maroon and White

Nickname: Aggies

Mascot: Reveille

Campus Attractions: George Bush Presidential Library and Museum, Bonfire Memorial, Texas A&M Sports Museum, Century Tree

Phone: 979-845-3211 (general information), 979-845-2345 (campus police), 979-845-5725 (athletic department)

Tickets: 888-TAM-12TH or www.12thmanfoundation.com

school with a stronger commitment to military training and more focus on agricultural and engineering studies. At the dawning of the twentieth century, Cadet life became the school's identity, and thousands of graduates would serve in World Wars I and II.

Before then, the school's first football team took shape in 1894, and the program first flourished under Coach Charley Moran, whose controversial style stoked a budding rivalry with Texas, to the extent the schools stopped playing from 1912 to 1914. The series resumed in 1915 with the birth of the Southwest Conference, and Texas A&M went on to win six league championships in eleven years under Dana X. Bible.

The rivalry with Texas extended beyond the football field. From its founding, Texas A&M always considered itself sovereign to the state university in Austin, but when oil was discovered on UT lands in the 1930s, A&M reluctantly agreed to become a branch of the state university system, with the purpose of taking home a third of the oil revenue that flowed through the state's Permanent University Fund.

The rivalry with Texas was renewed in football, too, and in 1939, under Coach Homer Norton, the Aggies won their only national championship, going 11-0 with fullback John Kimbrough plowing their path, punctuated by a 14-13 win over Tulane in the Sugar Bowl.

Other than a brief renaissance under Paul "Bear" Bryant from 1955 to 1957, the program had middling success until the 1980s. By then, the university had undergone unprecedented change under General James Earl Rudder. The school's sixteenth president oversaw the name change to Texas A&M University. Women and minorities were allowed to enroll as full-time students for the first time, and joining the Corps of Cadets became voluntary.

As the university grew in size and stature, the football program thrived in the latter years of the century, first under Jackie Sherrill, then R. C. Slocum, winning the Southwest Conference six times from 1985 to 1993 and developing new

PROGRAM HIGHLIGHTS

NATIONAL CHAMPIONSHIPS (1): 1939

SOUTHWEST CONFERENCE CHAMPIONSHIPS (17): 1917, 1919, 1921, 1925, 1927, 1939, 1940, 1941, 1956, 1967, 1975, 1985, 1986, 1987, 1991, 1992, 1993

BIG 12 CHAMPIONSHIPS (1): 1998

BIG 12 SOUTH CHAMPIONSHIPS (2): 1997, 1998

BOWL RECORD: 14-19 (.424). Last bowl—33-22 over Northwestern in 2011 Meineke Car Care Bowl of Texas

LONGEST WINNING STREAK: 19 games, 1939-40

WINNINGEST COACH: R. C. Slocum (1989 2002), 123-47-2, 72.1 percent

HEISMAN TROPHY WINNERS OR HIGHEST HEISMAN FINISH: Running back John David Crow, 1957 winner

traditions, like the 12th Man Kickoff Team and the Wrecking Crew defense. Slocum guided the Aggies into the Big 12 Conference in 1996 and captured the conference title two years later by stunning Kansas State in double overtime in the league championship game in St. Louis.

That would be the Aggies' high point in the Big 12 as Slocum's time ran out in 2002, and neither successors Dennis Franchione or Mike Sherman could recapture the glory. By 2011, A&M's frustrations with Texas and its Longhorn Network, a $300 million venture with ESPN, reached a boiling point as campus leaders sought refuge in the SEC. The marriage was enacted on September 27, and by season's end, the Aggies had a new coach to lead them into the new era, Kevin Sumlin, most recently the head coach at Houston and a former Aggies assistant.

LEGENDS

John Kimbrough

Texas A&M's 1939 national championship team was known for suffocating defense, but the bruising fullback from Haskell, Texas, known as "Jarrin' John" was the star on offense. Kimbrough finished fifth and second in the Heisman voting in 1939 and 1940.

Paul "Bear" Bryant

Of the five A&M coaches in the College Football Hall of Fame, Bryant lasted the least amount of years, coaching the Aggies from 1954 to 1957. But he might have left the strongest legacy with his initial preseason training camp in Junction, Texas, the inspiration behind the 2001 book *Junction Boys* and the ESPN film of the same name.

John David Crow

The Aggies' only Heisman winner played in only seven games because of injuries in 1957 and ran for only 562 yards but still managed to edge Iowa's Alex Karras in the voting. He returned to A&M in 1988 and served five years as athletic director.

Dat Nguyen

Easily the most decorated defensive player in A&M history, the son of Vietnamese refugees swept the Lombardi and Bednarik awards in 1998 and was the runner-up for the Butkus. He finished his career as A&M's career tackles leader with 517 stops.

HOME OF THE 12TH MAN

FIGHT SONG

"AGGIE WAR HYMN"

Hullabaloo, Caneck! Caneck!
Hullabaloo, Caneck! Caneck!
All hail to dear old Texas A&M,
Rally around Maroon and White,
Good luck to the dear old Texas Aggies,
They are the boys who show the real old fight.
That good old Aggie spirit thrills us.
And makes us yell and yell and yell;
So let's fight for dear old Texas A&M,
We're goin' to beat you all to
Chig-gar-roo-gar-rem!
Chig-gar-roo-gar-rem!
Rough! Tough! Real Stuff! Texas A&M!
Good-bye to Texas University.
So long to the Orange and the White.
Good luck to the dear old Texas Aggies,
They are the boys who show the real old fight.
'The eyes of Texas are upon you .'
That is the song they sing so well,
So good-bye to Texas University,
We're goin' to beat you all to
Chig-gar-roo-gar-rem
Chig-gar-roo-gar-rem
Rough! Tough! Real Stuff! Texas A&M!

STADIUM

Kyle Field: Voted college football's best home venue many times over, Kyle Field can be intimidating for both visiting players and media. Reporters making their first visit to Texas A&M's home stadium are in for a surprise when 80,000-plus Aggie fans break into the "Aggie War Hymn" and the press box sways from side to side along with the singing crowd. It's just one of the many game-day traditions at the stadium named after Edwin Jackson Kyle, the school's dean of agriculture and athletic council president who in 1904 fenced off a corner of campus where he built a grandstand that would become home to A&M's baseball and football teams. In 1927, the school agreed to build a new stadium, expanding Kyle's original structure into a horseshoe that seated 33,000. Kyle Field, home of the 12th Man, has undergone numerous expansion projects over the years and in the 1990s became one of the country's least hospitable venues: The Aggies went 55-4-1 at home for the decade.

MASCOTS

Before the Aggies won their lone national title, before Bear Bryant arrived on campus, before John David Crow captured the Heisman, there was Reveille, the beloved pooch and highest-ranking member of the Corps of Cadets. In 1931, some cadets were driving back from Navasota, Texas, when their car struck a black and white mutt. The cadets brought the dog back to campus, and as a bugler played "Reveille" the next morning, the dog perked up and started barking. A name and tradition were born.

The next football season, Reveille joined the marching band on the field for game days and became the team's official mascot. When Reveille died on January 18, 1944, the school gave her a formal military funeral on Kyle Field and buried her near the north entrance of the field, where she'd always be facing the scoreboard. Starting with Reveille III, all of the ensuing mascots have been purebred collies, including the current edition, Reveille VIII, who began her tour in August 2008.

NOTABLE ALUMS

Randy Barnes—Olympic shot putter

Robert Earl Keen—Country artist

Lyle Lovett—Singer-songwriter

Rick Perry—Texas governor

Stacy Sykora—Olympic volleyball player

Corps of Cadets Company E-2 is assigned to care for Reveille with a sophomore put in charge of her personal care. Given the rank of five-star general, Reveille wears five diamonds on the maroon and white blanket draped over her back on game days. According to campus lore, if Reveille falls asleep on a cadet's bed, the cadet must sleep on the floor. And if she barks in a classroom during a lecture, the class is dismissed.

MIZZOU CONNECTION

All-time football record vs. Missouri: 7-5

1957: Texas A&M 28, Missouri 0 (Columbia)
1958: Texas A&M 12, Missouri 0 (College Station)
1992: Texas A&M 26, Missouri 13 (Columbia)
1993: Texas A&M 73, Missouri 0 (College Station)
1998: Texas A&M 17, Missouri 14 (College Station)
1999: Texas A&M 51, Missouri 14 (Columbia)
2002: Missouri 33, Texas A&M 27, OT (College Station)
2003: Missouri 45, Texas A&M 22 (Columbia)
2006: Texas A&M 25, Missouri 19 (College Station)
2007: Missouri 40, Texas A&M 26 (Columbia)
2010: Missouri 30, Texas A&M 9 (College Station)
2011: Missouri 38, Texas A&M 31, OT (College Station)

Courtesy Mizzou Athletics Media Relations

Before he became a legend at Alabama, Bear Bryant toppled the Tigers as the coach at Texas A&M in 1957, the first of six consecutive Aggie wins over Missouri, including the 1993 mauling, the second-worst defeat in Tigers' history. But the losing stopped when Gary Pinkel took over at Mizzou. Starting with a dramatic OT win in College Station, Pinkel was 5-1 against the Aggies in Big 12 matchups, including three wins at Kyle Field—each time with a different quarterback. James Franklin delivered one of the series' most memorable plays in 2011, when he barreled through a swarm of Aggies on a twenty-yard touchdown run. "The true mark of a great quarterback is you guide your team to victory in a very difficult situation," Pinkel said of Franklin, who guides the Tigers back to Kyle Field in 2012—this time, in an SEC showdown.

Head of the class: Part of the SEC appeal for both Texas A&M and Missouri was their membership in the Association of American Universities, a prestigious invite-only collection of the country's top research universities. Texas A&M and Mizzou double the SEC's number of AAU members, joining Florida and Vanderbilt. Missouri was one of the first schools inducted into the organization in 1908, while Texas A&M is one of the newest members, receiving its invitation in 2001.

A Tiger becomes Bear: Bryant is best known for his time at Alabama, but a significant chapter in Bryant's legacy was born at Texas A&M. After taking over the Aggie program in 1954, Bryant put his new team through a brutal preseason training camp in Junction, Texas, an experience that inspired a book, Jim Dent's 2001 release *Junction Boys* and a made-for-TV movie by the same name. Playing the role of Bryant in the 2002 ESPN production was Mizzou grad Tom Berenger. "In the script, he's just as folksy and colorful as he was later in life," Berenger told ESPN.com when the movie first aired, "but he was much more intense at this time, and I was drawn to that intensity." Berenger came to MU to study journalism but switched to dramatic arts after starring in a campus production of *Who's Afraid of Virginia Woolf*. In 1988, he established a scholarship fund at MU's Department of Theatre.

GAME DAY

MEDIA

Broadcasting the Game: WTAW-AM 1620 and KZNE-AM 1150 in Bryan/College Station, Texas, KBME-AM 790 in Houston, and KJCE-AM 1370 and KKMJ-FM 95.5 in Austin

Covering the Aggies: www.AggieSports.com (*Bryan-College Station Eagle*), www.statesman.com/sports/aggies (*Austin American-Statesman*), www.chron.com/sports/aggies/ (*Houston Chronicle*), www.AggieYell.com (Rivals.com affiliate)

TAILGATING

A sea of maroon surrounds Kyle Field on game days as Aggieland is alive with tailgaters. Unless otherwise noted, site setup around Kyle Field can begin no earlier than noon on the day immediately preceding the game. Claiming unassigned tailgate areas before "setup day" is prohibited, and no overnight occupancy is allowed in tailgating areas. Tailgating sites open at 6:30 a.m. on game day and must be cleaned by midnight or three hours after the game, whichever's later. Tents and canopies must be secured and cannot obstruct sidewalks, driving lanes, or walkways. The same goes for furniture, grills, generators, or satellite dishes. Alcoholic beverages are prohibited in a few areas: the Memorial Student Center lawn, Simpson Drill Field, the All Faiths Chapel grounds, East of the Eagle in Cain Park, and Penberthy Intramural Fields. The school addresses all tailgating questions at tailgating.tamu.edu.

SHUTTLE

Texas A&M Transportation Services provides free express shuttles on game days from Post Oak Mall to Lubbock Street on the A&M campus. Shuttles begin two and a half hours before kickoff and run for two hours after the game. The shuttle stop at Post Oak Mall is in the Sears parking lot. A handicap-accessible shuttle service is available beginning three hours before kickoff and lasting ninety minutes after the game, originating from Lot 50. Three vans operate before and after the game, while one van operates during the game. The shuttle drops off in front of the Zone on Joe Routt Boulevard.

TRADITIONS

12th Man: Injuries left the Aggies so decimated in the 1922 Dixie Classic, Coach Dana X. Bible called former reserve player E. King Gill out of the press box and down to the sideline. Gill, an A&M basketball player, put on an injured Aggies uniform, and though he never entered the game, a proud tradition was born. "I wish I could say that I went in and ran for the winning touchdown, but I did not," Gill later famously said. "I simply stood by in case my team needed me." Over time the Corps of Cadets took on the role as the 12th Man, and the nickname has since come to describe the entire Aggie crowd.

Fightin' Texas Aggie Band: With meticulous precision, the country's largest military marching band has been parading through Aggie football games since the program's inaugural season in 1894. All three hundred-plus musicians are Corps of Cadets members.

Midnight Yell: Texas A&M has neither cheers nor cheerleaders. Aggies yell, and at midnight before every home game, they gather at Kyle Field to rehearse for the next day's production. The Aggie Yell Leaders, five males elected by the student body, lead the Fightin' Texas Aggie Band onto the field and conduct the show, using hand signals to call out the various yells and the singing of the "Aggie War Hymn" and "Spirit of Aggieland."

B-BALL, ETC.

The Aggies' men's basketball history is undistinguished at best. Shelby Metcalf won six Southwest Conference titles from 1964 to 1986, but after he was fired midway through the 1989-90 season, the Aggies went another sixteen years before making the NCAA Tournament during a renaissance under Billy Gillispie. In between were forgettable campaigns under Kermit Davis Jr., Tony Barone, and Melvin Watkins, who coached the Aggies to their first winless conference season since 1944. Gillispie won seventy games in three seasons at A&M with two NCAA Tournament appearances. The Aggies made four straight return trips to the NCAAs under Mark Turgeon but relapsed in 2011-12 under Billy Kennedy, posting their first losing season in eight years.

The women's basketball program has thrived recently under Gary Blair, winning two Big 12 Tournaments and the 2011 NCAA Tournament. Texas A&M has one of the country's most successful athletic departments in the non-revenue sports, owning national titles in softball, men's and women's track and field, men's golf, and equestrian.

ABOUT TOWN

The roots of College Station, Texas, are intertwined with the university as they grew together in the 1870s after the land-grant institution was founded in the desolate area of East Central Texas. The town was incorporated in 1938 and named after the local train depot. Paired with nearby Bryan, the Bryan/College Station metro area regularly posts unemployment figures among the lowest in Texas, and College Station is often listed among the most educated cities in America by *Money Magazine*. Bryan was established in 1859 and named after William Joel Bryan, a nephew of Texas pioneer Stephen F. Austin. Higher education is one of the area's top businesses as Bryan is home to two-year school Blinn College.

LODGING

Traditions Club: If you're looking for luxurious surroundings on your overnight stay, the fully furnished Cottages and Casitas on Aggieland's premier private golf club is the place. Traditions Club features a Jack Nicklaus–designed golf course, one of the best in Texas, and casual and fine dining choices. *3131 Club Dr., Bryan, TX 77807, 979-779-1007, www.traditionsclub.com*

Hilton College Station & Conference Center: Located just two miles from Texas A&M's campus, the Hilton features more than three hundred rooms and sixty-five suites, along with Bell Ranch Steakhouse, offering breakfast, brunch, lunch, happy hour, and dinner. *801 University Drive East, College Station, TX 77840, 979-693-7500*

The LaSalle Hotel: Selling itself on vintage charm with modern amenities, the LaSalle reopened its doors in 2000 and helped revitalize downtown Bryan. Among the amenities: complimentary breakfast, an evening beer and wine reception, and the hotel's signature bedtime cookie buffet. *120 South Main St., Bryan, TX 77803, 979-822-2000, www.lasalle-hotel.com*

EATING

Koppe Bridge Bar & Grill: Known for its mouth-watering burgers and rustic décor, Koppe Bridge reminds its customers, "This is Texas Paradise." *11777 Wellborn Rd., College Station, TX 77840, 979-764-2933; 3940 Harvey Rd., College Station, TX 77845, 979-776-2833, www.koppebridge.com*

C&J Barbecue: From its early days as a convenience store, Chip and Jo Manning's eatery has been serving up the area's signature flavors for more than a decade. For twelve years running, C&J has won the local Reader's Choice Award for the best BBQ in Brazos Valley. Their three locations cook 2,200 pounds of meat per day. *4304 Harvey Rd., College Station, TX 77840, 979-776-8969; 1010 South Texas Ave., Bryan, TX 77803, 979-822-6033; 105 Southwest Parkway, College Station, TX 77840, 979-696-7900, www.cjbbq.com*

SIGHTSEEING

Brazos Valley Museum of Natural History: The 9,400-square-foot museum features fossils, sculptures, antique farming equipment, and more than fifteen varieties of live animals and even more taxidermy mounts. *3232 Briarcrest Dr., Bryan, TX 77802, 979-776-2195, www.brazosvalleymuseum.org*

George Bush Presidential Library and Museum: Revisit the career of the forty-first president and discover artifacts, films, photos, and interactive video, plus a replica of his Camp David office and the White House Situation Room. *1000 George Bush Dr., College Station, TX 77845, 979-691-4000, www.bushlibrary. tamu.edu*

SHOPPING

Catalena Hatters: Sammy and Carolyn Catalena make it clear on their website: They don't carry belts, boots, jeans, or shirts—just their famous handmade custom-fitted cowboy hats. Catalena Hatters was the first custom hatter to sell the "Gus," made popular by Robert Duvall's character in Lonesome Dove. *203 N. Main St., Bryan, TX 77803, 800-976-7818, www.catalenahats.com*

Benjamin Knox Gallery: Known as the Texas Aggie Artist for his paintings, drawings, and photographs of iconic sights and scenes from around Aggieland, the Texas A&M graduate sells his work at the gallery, along with custom framing and wine by the bottle. *405 University Dr. East, College Station, TX 77840, 979-691-2787, www.benjaminknox.com*

NIGHTLIFE

The Dixie Chicken: Located across the street from Kyle Field, this A&M landmark calls itself College Station's most famous watering hole since 1974 and claims to serve the most beer per square foot of any bar in the country. *307 University Dr., College Station, TX 77840, 979-846-2322, www.dixiechicken.com*

Hurricane Harry's: College Station's home for Country Western music and live tunes. *313 College Ave., College Station, TX 77840, 979-846-3343, www.harrys. bcsclubs.com*

Fitzwilly's Bar & Grill: Check out live music on the patio or saddle up to a beer at the bar, but there's no shortage of games to play at this two-story hangout, from darts, pool, shuffleboard, washers, bean bags, dominoes to something called "Big Ass" Jenga. *303 University Dr., College Station, TX 77840, 979-846-8806, www.fitzwillysbar.com*

TRAVELING TO COLLEGE STATION?

Mizzou and A&M might be old conference cohorts, but they're not within driving distance. Your best bet is to fly into Austin or Houston and make the drive into College Station. Austin-Bergstrom International, Houston's George Bush Intercontinental, and Houston's Hobby are all roughly one hundred miles from A&M. The Mizzou Alumni Association hosts a Tiger Tailgate. Visit MizzouSportsTravel.com for more information on tickets and pricing.

THE MIZZOU FAN'S SURVIVAL GUIDE TO THE SEC

VANDERBILT

A $1 million donation these days is notable. Back in the spring of 1873 when a wealthy New Yorker, Commodore Cornelius Vanderbilt, wrote the check that created Vanderbilt University, the only private school in today's Southeastern Conference, it was outrageous.

The commodore was inspired by Methodist Bishop Holland N. McTyeire of Nashville. A cousin of the commodore's young second wife, McTyeire went to New York for medical treatment early in 1873 and spent time recovering in the Vanderbilt mansion.

Unlike many colleges, women were allowed to attend Vanderbilt almost from the outset, starting in 1875. By 1913, more than 20 percent of the student body was composed of women.

Vanderbilt's enrollment doubled every twenty-five years during the first century of the university's history. The campus size expanded to more than three hundred acres, and the university has consistently been ranked among the best in the nation academically.

Vanderbilt would love to obtain the same top twenty ranking in football, and there are

VANDERBILT UNIVERSITY

Students: 6,817

Nashville: pop. 601,222

Vanderbilt Stadium: seats 39,773

Colors: Black and Gold

Nickname: Commodores

Mascot: Mr. C (Mr. Commodore)

Campus Attractions: Commons Center, Bishop Joseph Johnson Black Cultural Center

Phone: 615-322-7311 (general information)
615-322-2745 (campus police)
615-322-GOLD (4653) (athletic department)

Tickets: 615-322-4653 or 877-44-VANDY (615-448-2639) or www.vucommodores.com/tIckets/vand-tickets.html

signs that may happen under Coach James Franklin, who in 2011 became the first Vandy coach in history to take his team to a bowl game. Franklin's mantra is "ignore the past." It's good advice, because a large majority of the Commodores' football past—probably six decades—has consisted of being drubbed, in large part to having more stringent academic standards than the majority of their opponents.

Vanderbilt's heyday was in the program's first sixty years, starting with the first game in 1890 through the 1940s. The Vanderbilt program picked up steam in 1904 when it hired Dan McGugin, nephew of famed University of Michigan coach Fielding H. Yost. McGugin coached thirty years at Vanderbilt until 1934, only missing the 1918 season to serve in World War I as a lieutenant colonel. His Vandy teams were dominant, with an average victory margin of 18.4 points. He retired because of health problems, just a couple of years after Vanderbilt had joined the new Southeastern Conference that began play in 1933.

The year after McGugin retired, Vanderbilt finished second in the SEC to champion LSU, and to this day that's still the Commodores' best finish in the league. As other SEC schools put more emphasis on its football programs, hiring better coaches and improving facilities, Vandy fell by the wayside. Heading into the 2012 season, Vandy has had forty-six losing seasons in the last fifty-two years, spanning thirteen different coaches. Incredibly, in thirty-six of those seasons, Vandy didn't win more than one league game. From 1976 to midway through the 1981 season, the Commodores lost thirty-three straight SEC games.

Gerry DiNardo, who coached at Vanderbilt from 1991 to 1994 and was 19-25 before being hired by LSU (despite losing 65-0 to Tennessee in his final game coaching the Commodores), said the biggest hurdle for Vandy traditionally is preventing players from mentally raising the white flag when seasons quickly turn sour. "The mentality of when things go bad with Vanderbilt football is, 'Hey, at the end of the day, we're smarter than everybody else, and we're

PROGRAM HIGHLIGHTS

NATIONAL CHAMPIONSHIPS (0):

SEC CHAMPIONSHIPS (0):

BOWL RECORD: 2-2-1 (.500). Last bowl—Lost 31-24 to Cincinnati in 2011 AutoZone Liberty Bowl

LONGEST WINNING STREAK: 20 games (twice), 1956-58

WINNINGEST COACH: Dan McGugin (1904-17, 1919-34), 197-55-19, 76.2 percent

HEISMAN TROPHY WINNERS OR HIGHEST HEISMAN FINISH: Center Carl Hinkle, 1937 seventh place

getting a better education,'" DiNardo says. "You might make an argument a Vanderbilt degree might be more prestigious than many other schools. But that doesn't give you an excuse to be bad in football. Losing has to become unacceptable." That's the attitude Vandy now hopes it has in Franklin, who in his first season in 2011 guided the Commodores to a 6-7 record and showed a feisty public willingness that Vanderbilt would not be bullied anymore.

"I'm a guy who has always had a chip on my shoulder," Franklin says. "I'm a blue-collar guy who has worked for everything he's ever gotten in life. I'm a fighter, and I don't like being disrespected. I don't like people talking down to me or people I care about."

LEGENDS

Dan McGugin

Winningest coach in school history, McGugin won eight or more games in eleven of thirty seasons (back when seasons didn't last more than nine or ten games).

Bill Wade

Quarterback Bill Wade was the SEC's 1951 Player of the Year and the only Vandy player ever taken No. 1 overall in the NFL draft, by Los Angeles in 1952.

Earl Bennett

The favorite target of then-Vandy quarterback Jay Cutler, Bennett is the SEC's all-time receptions leader with 236 in three seasons from 2005 to 2007.

Jim Arnold

Just one of five SEC punters in history named as an Associated Press first-team All-American in 1982, Arnold holds league career records for most punts (277 from 1979 to 1982) and most yards punted (12,171). With all that, he even averaged 43.9 yards.

NOTABLE ALUMS

Fred Thompson—Movie and TV actor and former U.S. senator from Tennessee

Lamar Alexander—Current U.S. senator from Tennessee, former Tennessee governor, and former U.S. Secretary of Education

Dr. Bernie Machen—President of the University of Florida since 2003

Dierks Bentley—Country music star with eight No. 1 records on Country chart

---

STADIUM

Vanderbilt Stadium: With just 39,773 seats, Vanderbilt Stadium is the smallest in the SEC. But the stadium, which opened in 1981 after being built in just nine months on the same site as the school's old stadium Dudley Field, has some advantages that stadiums three times larger don't enjoy. The intimate setting guarantees close sightlines. And the stadium is a block away from bustling West End Avenue, which is brimming with killer restaurants, bars, and shopping.

MASCOT

Since Commodore Cornelius Vanderbilt donated $1 million to start the university in 1873—he was obviously way ahead of his time in corporate branding—the school acquired the nickname the Commodores. In the mid-to-late nineteenth century, a commodore in the U.S. Navy was the commanding officer in a rank of ships. Therefore, Vanderbilt's costumed sideline mascot, known as "Mr. C"—short for Mr. Commodore—always dresses in nineteenth-century naval regalia, complete with cutlass and muttonchops. In relation to today's world, he sort of looks like an angry Cap'n Crunch, the character for which a Quaker Oats cereal is named.

FIGHT SONG

"DYNAMITE"

Dynamite, Dynamite,

when Vandy starts to fight.

Down the field with blood to yield,

if need be save the shield.

If victory's won, when battle's done,

then Vandy's name will rise in fame.

But, win or lose, the fates will choose,

And Vandy's game will be the same.

Dynamite, Dynamite,

when Vandy starts to fight!

V-A-N-D-Y . . . Vandy, Vandy, Vandy, Go, Go, Go!

MIZZOU CONNECTION

All-time football record vs. Missouri: 1-2-1

1895: Missouri 16, Vanderbilt 0 (Columbia)

1896: Missouri 24, Vanderbilt 10 (St. Louis)

1957: Missouri 7, Vanderbilt 7 (Nashville)

1958: Vanderbilt 12, Missouri 8 (Columbia)

Vanderbilt, the SEC's smallest and lone private school, will forever be part of Mizzou trivia. Dan Devine's first opponent as the Tigers' head coach? It was the Commodores, who came into Columbia in 1958 and earned their first win over MU in four tries, a series that started during both programs' infancy in the nineteenth century. The first matchup was a shutout for the Tigers under C.D. Bliss, a former star player at Yale who coached Missouri to a 7-1 record in his lone season, giving him the second-best winning percentage among the thirty-one men to coach the Tigers. "Vanderbilt never stood a ghost of a show to score, never having possession of the ball in Missouri's territory," wrote the MU yearbook, *The Savitar*.

Woeful Woody: In 1985, Missouri turned its program over to Robert "Woody" Widenhofer, a former Tiger linebacker and owner of four Super Bowl rings, all won as a Pittsburgh Steelers defensive assistant. Mizzou crafted the slogan "Hitch a ride on Woody's Wagon," but it couldn't stay out of the ditch: The Tigers went 1-10 his first season and won just twelve games in four years before Widenhofer resigned after the 1988 season. His .284 winning percentage is the worst in school history among coaches who lasted more than three years. In the 1990s, Widenhofer resurfaced at Vanderbilt, first as defensive coordinator and later head coach, a position he held from 1997 to 2001. His record wasn't much better in Nashville, just 15-40. His nine teams at Mizzou and Vandy were outscored by a combined 886 points.

Sportswriter U (times two): Missouri's vaunted School of Journalism has produced many a notable scribe, especially when it comes to covering sports. Missouri grads are scattered in press boxes all over the country during football season, including national columnists Pat Forde (Yahoo! Sports) and Dennis Dodd (CBS Sports). Other MU J-School grads include ESPN anchors John Anderson and Michael Kim, ESPN investigative reporter T. J. Quinn and former PBS anchor Jim Lehrer. Despite not offering a journalism degree, Vanderbilt might be the only SEC school that can compete with Mizzou when it comes to producing journalists. Grantland Rice, one of the most celebrated sportswriters of the twentieth century, graduated from Vanderbilt, as did his protégé, Fred Russell of the *Nashville Banner*. Among the notable writers who have won Vanderbilt's prestigious Russell-Rice Sports Writing Scholarship are Skip Bayless (ESPN), Tyler Kepner (*The New York Times*), Mark Bechtel and Lee Jenkins (*Sports Illustrated*), and Dave Sheinin (*The Washington Post*). ESPN's Buster Olney is also a Vandy grad.

GAME DAY

MEDIA

Broadcasting the Game: WRQQ-FM 97.1 (Nashville); KWAM-AM 99 (Memphis)

Covering the Commodores: www.tennessean.com/section/SPORTS0602/
Sports-Vanderbilt-Commodores (*The Tennessean Nashville*)

TAILGATING

Because Vanderbilt Stadium is completely surrounded by commercial property and other athletic facilities, there is virtually no place to tailgate. The Vanderbilt athletic department is marketing a small tailgate area on the corner of Jess Neely Drive and Natchez Trace outside the stadium available only to Vanderbilt season-ticket holders.

SHUTTLE

There is a lack of free parking close to the stadium—the only free parking is at Terrace Place and Wesley Garages just off of 21st Avenue, which is a fifteen- to twenty-minute walk through the heart of campus to Vanderbilt Stadium. There are NO shuttles.

TRADITIONS

The Admiral: That's the name for the naval horn that has been atop the Vanderbilt Stadium press box since 1993. It sounds during pre-game, minutes prior to kickoff to inform partying fans outside the stadium that the game is about to begin. It also blows when Vandy scores.

The Anchor: The Commodores began using an anchor in 2004 under Coach Bobby Johnson, who sought a symbol of strength and support for his program. Current Vandy coach James Franklin commissioned a special display case constructed for the Anchor to occupy year-round. The Anchor makes all road trips with Vanderbilt.

Victory Flag: During football season, if you don't know if Vanderbilt won or lost the previous Saturday, all you have to do is look above the west side of Vanderbilt Stadium, because each time after Vandy wins, a black flag is hoisted where it remains all week until the next game. This tradition began in 2004.

B-BALL, ETC.

Women's basketball (1993 Final Four) and baseball (a participant in the 2011 College World Series) have had brushes with winning a national championship. But women's bowling is the only sport in Vanderbilt athletic history to capture an NCAA national title. Since the program was established in 2004-05, the Vandy women (prior to the 2011-12 season) have finished fifth place or better in the national title tournament. That includes a national championship in 2007, third in 2008, and second in 2011.

ABOUT TOWN

Nashville was founded Christmas Eve 1779 by two groups of pioneer settlers, the first led by James Robertson. A few months later on April 24, 1780, Robertson and his party of men were joined by Colonel John Donelson, as well as the wives and children of the men who originally arrived with Robertson. For the first ten years, the settlement was called Nashborough before the name was changed to Nashville. Nashville was named the permanent capital of Tennessee in 1843. By 1900, the city had its first downtown skyscraper. In the 1940s and early 1950s, country music began exploding in Nashville to the point where it has now become the city's biggest tourist draw. And in the late 1990s, Nashville got its first major professional sports teams, the NFL's Tennessee Titans, transported from Houston where they had been the Oilers since 1960, and an NHL expansion team called the Predators.

LODGING

Marriott at Vanderbilt University: The most convenient hotel in the SEC in relationship to the football stadium, this Marriott looms over the north end of Vanderbilt Stadium. *2555 West End Ave., Nashville, TN 37203, 615-321-1300, www.marriott.com*

Gaylord Opryland Resort and Convention Center: If you want to catch some of the best of country music next door at the Grand Ole Opry, this 2,881-room hotel is the place to stay. *2800 Opryland Dr., Nashville, TN 37214, 615-889-1000, www.gaylordhotels.com/opryland*

The Hermitage Hotel: Nashville's grand old dame opened in 1910, and it never looked better. Richly appointed rooms, and fine dining on the premises at The Capitol Grille and Oak Bar. *231 6th Ave. N, Nashville, TN 37219, 615-244-3121 or 888-888-9414, www.thehermitagehotel.com*

EATING

Giovanni's: Put together a Florence, Italy-born-and-trained executive chef, a gracious and attentive wait staff, and a dazzling multi-leveled dining room with a grand stairway leading to the second level, and you have an exquisite Italian dining experience. *909 20th Ave. S, Nashville, TN 37212, 615-760-5932, www.giovanninashville.com*

Pancake Pantry: Sure, there's usually a line to get in this popular family-owned eatery that opened in 1961. Ninety-nine percent of the reason for the popularity is the chance to eat one of twenty kinds of pancakes topped by secret-recipe syrups. The other 1 percent is celebrity watching. Opens at 6 a.m. on all days that end in the letter "y." *1796 21st Ave. S, Nashville, TN 37212, 615-383-9333, www.thepancakepantry.com*

Noshville: An honest-to-goodness New Yawk deli in the heart of twang-twang land? It's true and it's spectacular. Homemade soups, thick sandwiches with fresh meats and cheeses, homemade meat loaf so good it's a religious experience. Four locations around Nashville, but the original is the truth. *1918 Broadway, Nashville, TN 37203, 615-329-6674, www.noshville.com*

SIGHTSEEING

Country Music Hall of Fame: Located almost directly behind Bridgestone Arena in downtown Nashville, this is simply one of the finest music halls of fame in the world. Admission starts at $20 for general admission. *222 5th Ave. S, Nashville, TN 37203, 615-416-2001, www.countrymusichalloffame.org*

Grand Ole Opry: The biggest names in country music, past and present, perform a two-hour show every Friday and Saturday, broadcast live on the radio. Tickets range from $55 to $24. *2804 Opryland Dr., Nashville, TN 37214, 615-871-OPRY (6779), www.opry.com*

The Hermitage: The original home of President Andrew Jackson, constructed about 1820, opened as a museum in 1889 and restored in the 1990s, this mansion still has many of Jackson's original furniture pieces and family possessions. *4580 Rachel's Lane, Nashville, TN 37076, 615-889-2941, www. thehermitage.com*

SHOPPING

Hillsboro Village: Three miles southwest of downtown skirting the border of Vanderbilt, this neighborhood has a collection of off-the-beaten-path stores and eateries. So browse through a bookstore like BookManBookWoman (*1713 21st Ave. S, www.bookmanbookwoman.com*), and then eat a gourmet hot dog at The Dog of Nashville (*2127 Belcourt Ave., www.thedogofnashville.com*).

Cool Springs Galleria: The city of Nashville expanded south to such suburbs as Brentwood, Franklin, and Cool Springs, which has a dynamite 165-store mall anchored by Macy's, Dillard's, and Sears. Take Interstate 65 South out of Nashville to Exit 69.

NIGHTLIFE

Tootsie's Orchid Lounge: The biggest names in country music cut their musical chops in this historic honky-tonk. And you never know who's going to drop in, such as Kid Rock in January 2012 for a four-hour set. *422 Broadway, Nashville, TN 615-726-0463, www.tootsies.net*

Bluebird Café: An unassuming one hundred-seat venue in a strip mall where three or four songwriters seated in the center of the café take turns playing their songs and accompanying each other. Again, this is a place where you might see the next Garth Brooks, who was discovered at the Bluebird by Capitol Records. *4104 Hillsboro Pike, Nashville, TN 37215, 615-383-1461, www. bluebirdcafe.com*

Sam's All-American Sports Grill: Voted Nashville's best sports bar for two consecutive years by readers of *Nashville Scene Magazine* and named by *Maxim Magazine* as one of the top sixteen sports bars in the country to watch a game. The bar is smoke-free. *1803 21st Ave. S, Nashville, TN 37212, 615-383-3601, www. samssportsgrill.com*

TRAVELING TO NASHVILLE?

It's a doable drive from St. Louis, roughly five hours on I-64, I-57, and finally I-24 into Nashville. Otherwise, direct flights are available to Nashville International, from both Kansas City and St. Louis. The Mizzou Alumni Association hosts a Tiger Tailgate. Visit MizzouSportsTravel.com for more information on tickets and pricing.